RELIGION AND DHARMA

RELIGION AND DHARMA

BY

SISTER NIVEDITA

(MARGARET E. NOBLE)

GYAN

Published by

Gyan Publishing House
5, Ansari Road
Daryaganj, New Delhi-110002
Phone: 011-47034999, 9811692060
E-mail: books@gyanbooks.com

Distribution Network
gyanbooks.com
India, USA, Canada, UK, Australia

ISBN: 978-81-212-7025-0 (PB)
First Published, 1915

2nd Impression 2024

Printed at: Gyan Press, Delhi.

RELIGION AND DHARMA
Author: SISTER NIVEDITA

RELIGION AND DHARMA

RELIGION AND DHARMA

BY

SISTER NIVEDITA

(MARGARET E. NOBLE)

WITH A PREFACE BY S. K. RATCLIFFE

LONGMANS, GREEN AND CO.

39 PATERNOSTER ROW, LONDON

FOURTH AVENUE & 30TH STREET, NEW YORK

BOMBAY, CALCUTTA, AND MADRAS

1915

PREFACE.

FROM an early stage of her life in India Sister Nivedita was closely in touch with the student community, especially in Bengal where her work lay. She was at the call of almost any group, so long as she was satisfied that there were sincere seekers among them, and her influence spread widely and rapidly, alike through her public addresses, which were eagerly welcomed, and through the exercise of her personal sympathy and counsel. When "The Web of Indian Life" was published, in 1904, the enthusiasm of the national movement was rising in Young India. Sister Nivedita was among the most forceful and devoted of its spiritual leaders, and the services of her voice and pen were in demand from every side. So far as the exacting claims of other work permitted, she yielded to requests for newspaper and magazine articles, and produced a good deal of occasional writing, besides more laborious studies which first appeared in the magazines. She gave cordial encouragement to such ventures of educational journalism as the *Modern Review* of Calcutta, then as now directed by Mr. Ramananda Chatterjee. To the pages of this admirable monthly she contributed the greater part of the papers afterwards collected in "Studies from an Eastern Home" and practically the whole of those in the "Footfalls of Indian History." At the same time she was writing, month by month, in the editorial columns of the *Modern Review* a series of notes and brief articles suggested chiefly by the ethical and religious aspects of the advancing national movement. It is from those pieces that the present volume has been compiled.

None saw more clearly than Sister Nivedita, from the beginning, the possibilities and the perils of Indian nationalism as then understood and preached. There were many, both Indian and European, to insist upon the difficulties, or the futility, of the nationalist conception and aim ; to argue that it was but one more expression of the chaos wrought by the working of the West upon the East. The confusion was not to be denied ; but Sister Nivedita had no doubt as to the capacity of the Indian mind and character to emerge. To her, the striking characteristic of the Transition was the speed with which, in the nineteenth century, the ancient social order of India had adjusted itself to the demands of a modern alien civilization. The later steps should be not more, but less, difficult since they would be conscious and controlled. They must, in Sister Nivedita's view, be taken by India itself. There could, she held, be no question as to the power of the Indian consciousness to absorb the contribution of the West and to transmute it; and the way to that she saw through an exchange of organic ideals between East and West. For India it would mean a renascence of *Dharma :* in other words, a re-interpretation in modern terms of the faith and practice of the past; a fresh relation of the contemplative to the active life; a new conception of worship and of sacrifice to the ideal; the monastic ideal expressed in social service; the recovery of the civic sense, and its re-establishment in a fuller understanding of the Indian social order ; the exaltation of work, of positive character, and of knowledge, in which alone could lie the mastery of the future.

Such is the theme of these papers. In fairness to the memory of the author, and for their right understanding, they should be read with a recollection of the circumstances amidst which they were thrown off —with great rapidity in the midst of a crowded and arduous life of service in India. The reader will not fail to remark, as an illustration of the completeness with which Sister Nivedita identified herself with India and its spirit, her constant use of "we" and "ours".

Some readers may wonder at the implied antithesis in the title between an English and a Sanskrit word which are frequently taken to be practically identical in meaning. *Dharma*, however, is a word that to the Hindu has a larger and more complex significance than that of Religion as commonly used among us. It includes the whole social conception of law and conduct and worship. *Dharma* is the force or principle that binds together; the union of traditional thought and faith, of common custom, loyalty, and understanding, that makes of society an organic or religious unity. "This patience, this steadfastness, this sincerity," Sister Nivedita wrote, "is *Dharma*—the substance, the self-ness, of things and of men."[1] She preferred to translate the word as the National Righteousness, and on the whole perhaps that is as close to an equivalent term in English as we may hope to achieve.

Viscount Haldane, in the address delivered before the American Bar Association in 1913,[2] has some remarks on the principle of Higher Nationality which bear upon the matter. Law, in the greater sense, he said, imports something more than the code of rules laid down by the State; it has a relation to the obligations of conscience and the General Will of Society. The field of individual conduct is covered, in the case of the citizen, only to a small extent by legality on the one hand and the dictates of the individual conscience on the other. "There is a more extensive system of guidance which regulates conduct and which differs from both in its character and sanction." Lord Haldane continues:—

In the English language we have no name for it, and this is unfortunate, for the lack of a distinctive name has occasioned

[1] P. 51. [2] "Higher Nationality," London: John Murray, 1913.

confusion both of thought and of expression. German writers have, however, marked out the system to which I refer and have given it the name of *Sittlichkeit*. . . . *Sittlichkeit* is the system of habitual customary conduct, ethical rather than legal, which embraces all those obligations of the citizen which it is "bad form" or "not the thing" to disregard.

Sitte is the German for custom, and *Sittlichkeit* implies custom and a habit of mind and action; let us say, the blend of social morality and social sanction embodying the ideal of the conduct of people towards each other and towards the community to which they belong.

Without such conduct and the restraints which it imposes there could be no tolerable social life, and real freedom from interference would not be enjoyed. It is the instinctive sense of what to do and what not to do in daily life and behaviour that is the source of liberty and ease. And it is this instinctive sense of obligation that is the chief foundation of society. Its reality takes objective shape and displays itself in family life and in our other civic and social institutions. It is not limited to any one form, and it is capable of manifesting itself in new forms and of developing and changing old forms. Indeed the civic community is more than a political fabric. It includes all the social institutions in and by which the individual life is influenced—such as are the family, the school, the church, the legislature, and the executive. None of these can subsist in isolation from the rest; together they and other institutions of the kind form a single organic whole, the whole which is known as the Nation.[1]

Sister Nivedita would have accepted every word of this exposition as covering a great part of the life of citizenship. And she would have added, with truth, that *Dharma* is a finer and more satisfying word for the living principle of conduct and society—finer and more satisfying in the measure of the infinitely more rich and profound conception which the Indian has of religion than the conception reached by the people from whom Lord Haldane borrowed his word.

S. K. R.

LONDON, *August*, 1915.

[1] "Higher Nationality," p. 23.

CONTENTS.

CONTENTS

RELIGION AND DHARMA.

EVERY religion centres round some particular idea: Ancient Egypt round death; Persia round the mystery of Good and Evil; Christianity round the redeeming love of a divine Incarnation. Only Hinduism aims at the heights of *Vairagyam* and *Mukti*, and at nothing secular. This is indeed the weak point of Hinduism. The quality by which Hinduism has it in her power to make up for this defect of her greatness, is her capacity for synthetizing every religious idea with which she comes in contact. The absorptive power of Hinduism as a religion, coupled with its resistant power as a civilization, furnishes one of the most startling paradoxes in the history of man. Derived originally from a veritable network of religions, in which the co-ordinating element was the philosophy now known as Vedanta, it has thrown out reforming sects in the Mohammedan period, and thrown out reforming sects in the Christian period, each of these being in fact the expression of its admiration for the new ideal of which it has caught a glimpse.

To-day, however, Hindus see that the greatest call upon the religious instincts of the country lies in the need of assimilating whole new areas of life. We must make possible the "short views" of the Christians. There must be some religious teaching and encouragement for those who only want heaven, not *Mukti.* There must be a recognition of *righteousness*, as well as of holiness. Righteousness lies in duty done: holiness requires renunciation. A thousand good citizens are necessary, as the background of one great *sannyasin.* There must then be a philosophy of citizenship, as well as of *Sannyas.*

And in truth the exaltation of one thing does not demand the decrying of its fellow. The ideal is always infinite, always divine. A highly moralized society produces the greatest saints. The purity of fathers and mothers makes possible the birth of Avatars. Where marriage is faithfully kept, there sincere *Sannyas* is possible, not amongst profligates and riotous livers. Similarly, the presence of honourable citizens is necessary to the maintenance of a grand religious ideal, and the citizen is as necessary to its manifestation as the monk.

But if this is so, we have to search our ancient scriptures with a new aim. We must seek for all that can support and encourage us in doing manfully the work of this present world. Renunciation can be achieved through duty quite as well as by the abandonment of duty. We have thousands of texts to tell us so, but the prevailing preconception in favour of *Sannyas* has led to our ignoring all that favours *Dharma.* The weak point of European society lies in the absence of the monastic ideal. True. But equally sure is it that the weak point of Hinduism is the want of emphasis on the ideal of the householder and the citizen. The reason lies largely in the fact that when our texts were formulated our society was as rich in virtue as in material resources. When the last of these deserts us, it is difficult to prevent the decay of the former; and what is wanted to-day is a deliberate recapture of both.

For this, we must exalt work. We must look upon the world as a school, in which it is worth while to strive for promotion from class to class. We must set our shoulder to the wheel and struggle unceasingly to attain the end we have set before ourselves. Our philosophy tells us that absolute progress is impossible in the things of this life. But relative progress is fully possible; and while we move on this plane of relativity, we must work as if perfection would reward the very next step.

Let us set before ourselves the master-ideals, even in things relative. "I do not make good screws, sir, I make the best that can be made," said an indignant workman in reply to too casual an inquiry. This ought to be our attitude. We must make the best screws that can possibly be made. In every direction it must be the same. The best not too good, the highest not too difficult, for us to attain. Nothing less than the utmost. Nothing easy. Nothing cheap. The same energy that might have made an ascetic will also make a workman, if that will better serve the Mother's purpose.

And let our ideals be higher for our friends also. Let no man consort with mean company. Monk or citizen, let a man be noble. Whether Brahman or pariah, let him practise self-respect, and demand the like from others. We help no one by being so passive as to convert him into a brute!

In the school, the lessons are graduated, but all alike are EDUCATION. All are equally the concern of the school-authorities. Even so with our civilization. The integrity of the man of business is to the full as acceptable an offering as the renunciation of the monk, for unless there be honest men of the world, the religious orders must come to an end.

Thus Hinduism, fully recognizing the need of the practical and secular life, and drawing from within herself the stores that are necessary for its development and growth, synthetizes once more ideals that seemed opposite. The super-social life is seen in its true relation to society. The goal is preached as attainable, not only by the sadhu in the forest, but also by the butcher in the town and the wife in the home.

MUKTI: FREEDOM.

OF all the questions that a wakeful and fresh intellect will constantly ask, there is none, perhaps, more sure to recur than, What is Freedom? Many of us are born struggling for actual freedom, for our own freedom. All of us are born to struggle for something. Nothing more terrible could be imagined than a human being put into circumstances so artificial that all motive for struggle was eliminated, and he was deprived of the natural human right of something to desire and strive for. We can imagine a man in prison for life realizing such hopelessness, though, if so, it must be because his whole conception of activity is social or muscular, and therefore can be thwarted. Or a cage made of riches, or rank,—such a cage as that of royal birth, for instance,—might produce this effect on a nature too good to lose itself in fleshly delights, and too stupid to find paths of self-development. But if so, the man who never struggled would grow up an idiot. That at least is certain. All our vivacity, all our intelligence, is developed by struggle. Only shapeless incapacity could result from its lack.

It has been said that the great may be distinguished from the little by whether or not they are struggling for freedom. This may be true. For there is no doubt that we may struggle for, and even realize, a thing which we could not possibly define intellectually.

Most of us win our own freedom in this thing and that thing, and thus gradually build up a more or less perfect freedom. Many struggle for freedom under the name of the Right. "God and my Right"—*Dieu et mon droit*—is a formula that refers to some such contest of the soul. It is only Hinduism that has been subtle enough to recognize that beyond the thing itself which seems to be the object of our strife, the real thirst of the soul is for *freedom*—and that this freedom is the essential condition of self-development. The man who is free, says *Dharma*, is the only man who is himself. The man who is really and fully himself is free—free in all directions, free of all bonds.

One essential characteristic of freedom is that it has always to be realized in opposition to something. The struggle of every individuality—whether a simple or a compound—is to define itself, by attaining self-direction, by repudiating the control of its fellow-organisms. Freedom from the pressure of his social surroundings is an absolute necessity of manly men. The manly man may choose to act precisely as his society would desire, but he must believe that he does this because he himself chooses, and not because society compels. And yet any great anxiety on this point is crude enough, since manly men are too accustomed to their own freedom, and their own power of defending their freedom, to be uneasy about it, or suspicious of invasions upon it. It is only a child, who has never yet felt himself grown-up, who finds it necessary to refuse whatever is asked of him, in order that he may hug to himself his own liberty of refusal. And here we note the vanity, the selfishness, the pre-occupation with self, and indifference to the needs of others, that make such natures, at such a stage, unfit for high and arduous forms of co-operation. The really great are born with such assurance of their own freedom to withhold, that they are full of eagerness to *give*, and welcome every opportunity of serving as a privilege. Such natures we see every day. Unselfishness is not rare amongst human beings. On the contrary, it is the mortar that joins the bricks of the whole edifice.

Society, then, is one of the forces against which the individual has to realize his own freedom—one of the powers from which he has to wrest it. But the question again occurs, what *is* that freedom for which the individual is struggling? And here arises one of the supreme fallacies. Some take it that freedom is identified with slavery to their own impulses. This is the freedom that makes drunkards, gluttons, and libertines.

At first, all our activity, all our development of faculty, depends upon desire: afterwards, desire is seen as a form of disease, of which we must be cured! Is this the truth? The momentum of desire, that impels us to yield inevitably to our own caprices, is not freedom. It is the last and subtlest form of bondage, the more dangerous and deadly for the fact that we are liable to mistake its nature. Liberty to realize what is our own will may be an essential condition of freedom, but until we are as free from that will, and the desires suggested by that body and mind, as from those of all the other hundreds of millions of human beings, we do not know what real freedom is.

How large, how calm, how full of exquisite joy and graciousness, never dimmed, is the heritage of life that awaits the individual in those elysian fields of the soul, where this freedom has been won! It may be manifested in any way, by any means. For only the free can apprehend what freedom is. Only the free can determine how freedom shall be shown. Only the actions of the free are potent, unhampered by feebleness of their own or aggression of others—free! free! Freedom is indeed the supreme good of the soul. So far from being "a night in which all cows are black," it is, as every Hindu knows, the perfect access of daylight, neither too much nor too little, into every nook and cranny of our universe. But even so, when we seek to define it, we are met by an eternal impossibility, and can only ejaculate "*Neti! neti!* Not this! Not this!"

The soldier has to learn that obedience is his form of prayer. To be doing *japam* when one ought to be resting, and consequently to be sleepy when one ought to be at work, is not a meritorious condition. No *punya* that way! The sunny-heartedness of the child, on the other hand, ready to forget all about its mother, if its mother tells it to run away and play, is true *bhakti*, and better than many *pranâms*.

Manliness may often prove to be the whole of piety! Some races have practised such virtue out of sheer instinct, but never before was a survey of life so comprehensive, so far-reaching, added to the treasury of authoritative pronouncements on religious truth. This manliness-which-is-righteousness involves, it will be noticed, a kind of *Mukti*, for the manly man has no time to be conscious of his own manliness. Heroism in great moments is the natural blossom of a life that in its little moments is fine and fearless.

THE GREATER RITUAL.

SO far from remaining unchanged, a religion that is alive must be always growing. Only the dead can be petrified in rigid forms. The living must be constantly assimilating new forces, new materials, responding in fresh ways to unprecedented stimuli, tending in some degree to remake the very environment that is re-moulding itself.

Even of the *Sanathan Dharma* this is true. Hinduism would not be eternal, were it not constantly growing and spreading, and taking in new areas of experience. Precisely because it has this power of self-addition and re-adaptation, in greater degree than any other religion that the world has ever seen, we believe it to be the one immortal faith, the great tree-stem, bearing on itself, as outlying branches, all the more fugitive creeds of the world.

It is necessary, however, to know in what direction to look for changes, if we would be intelligent about recognizing these when they come. Like Roman Catholicism, Hinduism has gone on for the last twelve hundred years developing more and more into a religion of segregation, the culture of the soul, a secret between the worshipper and the priest, or the soul and God. Undoubtedly it has been true, in this respect, to the ultimate message of all religions. The emancipation of the soul—Spiritual Individualism, as the Swami Vivekananda called it—is the main business of organized creeds. A few social benedictions are a mere side-issue.

But religion has also a communistic side. It lifts the soul to God, but it also binds together man and man. If we are the children of the Mother, we must for that very reason be brothers of one another. A specialization in one direction requires to be corrected by a compensating development in the other. More souls will now be emancipated by attention paid to the democratic or communistic side of worship.

For this, there will have to be common prayer. And common prayer itself must be organized. That is to say, there must be services in which responses are required from several worshippers at once, and these responses should be in the vernacular. When *slokas* are recited by a great number all together, it will be found desirable to divide these into two sections, and let them repeat the texts in antiphon.

The religious uses of the procession must be restored. We cannot doubt when we study Buddhism,—which was, of course, only a version of an older Hinduism,—that the procession, with banners, shanks, drums, incense, and holy water, was a great feature in old Indian worship. A few of its most beautiful uses still remain, as when seven women carry torches round the bridegroom, or the sons encircle the dead father with fire.

There ought now to be an anxious scrutinizing of these old ritual observances, and of the whole subject of ritual in general. Many of our own most lovely rites are still practised in Europe, though lost to us. We must restore the greater meanings of our Hindu ceremonies. Worship is in the future to have a place for the people, as well as for the priest. There is to be co-operation and self-organization, even in the praising of God.

THE CROWN OF HINDUISM.

We have heard much, lately, more or less sincere, about the Crown of Hinduism. But how many Hindus have themselves any idea of what is in fact the crown of their faith? If it really deserves all the good things said of it, it will not succumb, we may be sure, to the attacks of a foreign religion. The fact that such a fate can be foretold for it, with smiles, ought to be an indication to us of how much is meant by an empty compliment. The fact is, foreigners with all their perspicacity, cannot easily or actually distinguish between our religion and our social system, bound up as that is with a network of semi-religious sanctions. But our whole social system might conceivably disappear without in any degree affecting the most distinctive and important of our religious ideas. They are indeed as applicable to the West as to the East. Perhaps the real crown of Hinduism lies in the fact that it, almost alone amongst formulated faiths, has a section devoted to absolute and universal truths, and has no fear whatever of discriminating between these and such accidental expressions as might be confounded by the superficial with their belief itself.

In spite of its seemingly vast mythology, the actual content of Hinduism is infinitely less dependent on mythological ideas than any other religion whatsoever. He who is driven to abandon the historicity of Western beliefs has but sorry ground henceforth to stand upon. Not so the Hindu. There is no shade of the search after truth that is not looked upon here as religious heroism. We are in no danger of persecuting a man for no better reason than that he can see farther and deeper than we! Giordano Bruno would never have been burnt, Galileo would never have been put to the torture, if India had been their home and birthplace. The *Sanathan Dharma* sanctions and endorses every form of honest striving after knowledge. It is jealous and suspicious of no form of truth. Perhaps in this lies the true crown of Hinduism.

Ours is the religion of a people who have never relapsed into barbarism, and have never had any quarrel with education. We do not distinguish between the sacredness of different forms of truth. Truth is truth. We are not really so seriously incommoded by our mythology as those are who call us idolatrous by theirs. We must be true to what we believe. All knowledge is sacred. In the trust that has been snatched from the abyss, it is not for us to say what is more and what less binding. Mathematics is also God's. Men of science are also *rishis*.

We can afford to laugh at our foreign friends, in the fashions that sweep across their religious horizon. God really exists, the Westerns are inclined to believe, because a leading scientific man says so. This is mere childishness. Do they expect others to accept a religion whose own sons do it so little justice as this? To the Hindu, religion is experience or nothing. If science is also experience, he does not feel it incumbent upon him to deny either of two things, both of which he knows to be true. Is God in his keeping? Does the universe depend upon his immediate understanding of it? If he were a criminal judge he might have to exercise more humility and patience than this!

Hinduism never tends to make men contented to read or to believe. To have a right to talk, a man must first realize. No counterfeit coin will be accepted for this. We know the difference at sound between the spurious and the real. We can tell who speaks with authority and who as the scribes. Our faith rests from first to last on a basis of experience, of realization, of personal appropriation. Without this, a mere lip-adhesion is of no consequence in our eyes. Let it come, let it go. It does not count. Were the whole of our system of scaffolding to be swept away to-morrow, we should be able to reconstruct it all again: nay, we should be compelled to do so, out of the very wants of the human heart.

Let those who are disposed to wail by the river-side, shedding false tears over our approaching extinction, take heed lest it be not their own superstitions that are at the point of death instead of ours! Hinduism is not going to die because her sons have learnt to drink a cup of morning tea, forsooth! Caste, and occupation, and mode of living, and forms of culture might all disappear, and Hinduism remain intact as ever. In fact, is not something of the kind to be expected in the speedy spread of Hinduistic ideas to Christian lands? Our religion is fully compatible with any of the higher forms of civilization. But it will never die out of the land of its birth. If anything were needed to make this more certain, it would be just such ill-considered and premature exultation as that to which we have been alluding. Do we not know that with the passing of characteristic faiths comes the death of nations? Are we fools, that we should not know the meaning of the tale of contemporary civilizations in Ancient Egypt, and in Babylon, dead beyond power to revive, because they parted with their ancestral trust of thought? India shall not do this! Rather shall she go out into all the world, and see the inadequacy of more childish faiths met out of her own brimming store. Rather shall she become the Guru and instructor of all others, and learn to measure the greatness of her own thinkers by the littleness and shallowness of those who oppose them. Rather shall her pride and confidence in this her own treasure wax greater day by day. Smiling serenely, she will pass over her flatterers, her hypocritical sympathisers and her well-intentioned but foolish children easily elated by meaningless words, and let her own glance rest, in calm and content, on a future not far distant when the positions shall be reversed.

That such a time is coming, nay, that it is close at hand, we should be strangely disloyal to our Mother-Church to doubt. We should be strangely incompetent readers of her past triumphs, if we could not see. Not the churches of the world alone, but the very universities of Europe, will yet do homage before the names of Indian thinkers, who, living in the shelter of forest-trees, and clad in birch-bark or in loin-cloths, have formulated truths more penetrating and more comprehensive than any of which Europe herself—childishly bent on material comfort—ever dreamed.

HINDUISM AND ORGANIZATION.

HINDUISM is one of the finest and most coherent growths in the world. Its disadvantages arise out of the fact that it is a growth, not an organization; a tree, not a machine. In an age in which the whole world worships the machine, for its exactness, its calculableness, and its dirigibility, this fact, while it makes for a greater permanence, also involves a certain number of desiderata. The fruits of the tree of Hinduism are of an excellence unparalleled; but it is not easy to reach by its means those benefits that do not occur spontaneously, ends that have to be foreseen and deliberately planned and arranged for. For instance, alone amongst the world's faiths perhaps, ours has no quarrel of any sort with truth. Under its sway, the scientific mind is absolutely free to pursue to the uttermost its researches into the Infinite Nescience of things, the philosopher is encouraged to elucidate his conclusions, and simple piety does not dream of passing judgment on things admittedly too high for it. All this is true of Hinduism. At the same time, what has it done *to grasp* the highest scientific education for its children, or to impel its people forward upon the pursuit of mastery in learning or in ministering to social service?

There is nothing in Hinduism to forbid an attempt

on our part to compass these things, and the only thing that could drive us to make the effort,—namely a vigilant and energetic sense of affairs, a public spirit that took account of things as a whole,—was undoubtedly indicated by the Swami Vivekananda, as part of what he meant by Aggressive Hinduism. We ought to make our faith aggressive, not only internationally, by sending out missionaries, but also socially, by self-improvement; not only doctrinally, by accepting converts, but also spiritually, by intensifying its activity. What we need is to supplement religion by public spirit,—an enlightened self-sense in which every member of the community has a part. Class-preference is obsolete in matters of education. The career of the intellect is now for him who has the talent. By us, this principle has to be boldly and enthusiastically accepted. Even as the school is open to all, so must every form of social ministration be made. The college, the orphanage, the hospital, the women's refuge, these must be opened by such as have the devotion and energy for the task, and nothing must be said of the birth of the servant of humanity. By virtue of his consecration, he becomes a saint, even as, by his *jnânam*, the philosopher makes himself a *rishi*.

Activity is eased and heightened if it is socialized: that is to say, if it is the work of a body, espousing a common conviction, and not of a solitary individual, wandering the world, and divided between his idea itself and the question of its support. This common conviction, driving into work, is the reason why small religious sects are so often the source of vast movements of human amelioration. Many of these outstanding problems of Hinduism have been attacked, for instance, by the Brahmo Samaj, with considerable success. The little church forms a background and home for the worker. It sends him out to his task, rejoices over his success, and welcomes him back with laurels, or with ministration, when he turns home to die. Without some such city of the heart, it is difficult to see how the worker is to keep up his energy and courage. The praise and pleasure of our own little group of beloved ones is very sweet to all of us, and quite properly spurs us on to surmount many an obstacle that we should not otherwise attempt. Let the soul grow, by saying "not this! not this!" to what height it will; but let it *have* the occasion for practising this discrimination.

We must take up our problems, then, as social groups. Let no man enter on the apostolate that is to shake the world, alone. Everything done, every discovery made, even every poem written, and every dream dreamed, is a *social* achievement. Society has contributed to it, and will receive its benefits. Let the missionary, then, on whom the effort seems to rest, not reckon himself to be the chief actor. There must be some two or three, knit together by some well-wrought bond, in every undertaking that is to benefit humanity. Perhaps they were comrades at school and college. Perhaps they are disciples of a single master. Possibly they belong to the same village. Maybe they are fellow-workmen in some common employment. Whatever be the shaping force, there must be association of aim and co-operation of effort, if there is to be success, and there must be a strong bond of love amongst those few ardent souls who form the central core.

Voluntary association, the desire of a body to take on corporate individuality, is thus the point of departure within Hinduism for civic activity. But we must not forget how much every activity owes to the general movement of society around it. Work must be done by the few as the servants, not as the enemies, of the many. Every single movement needs other counter-movements to supplement it, if it is to maintain itself in vigour. Thus, the difficulty about technical education in India is not want of funds, which have been poured in in abundance; but want of general industrial development, in the society around. There is a fixed ratio between education and development which cannot be passed, hence only by definite and alternating increments to the one and to the other can progress take place. Again, there is a fixed proportion between the total of these and the community's need of the highest scientific research, which cannot be contravened. And all these alike must find themselves inhering in an inclusive social energy, which takes account of its own needs, its own problems and its own organs. The vivifying of this general social sense is the first of all our problems. We have to awaken it, to refresh it, and to keep it constantly informed. What this social sense has now first and foremost to realize, is our want of education, the need of a real ploughing of the mind. For this, high and low, we ought to be content to starve and slave and bear the utmost pinch of poverty. And not for our own sons alone. This is a matter in which the interest of all should be the interest of each one, the necessity of one the interest of all. We have to energize our culture. We have to learn to think of things in their wholeness, and to see them from new points of view. We have to possess ourselves of all that is known by humanity, not to continue in contentment with a mere corner of its knowledge, well fenced off. Are we mentally capable of science, of sanity, of comprehensiveness? If so, we have now to prove our capacity.

And where shall we find the starting-point for this new assault on the citadel of our own ignorance? Let us find it boldly amongst religious forces. In Buddhist countries, the monastery is the centre round which are grouped schools, libraries, museums, and efforts at technical education. Why should we not, in our Southern cities expect the temple, similarly, to take the lead, in the fostering of the new and higher education? Why should we dread the Brahman's tendency to exclusiveness and reaction? If it be really true that we are capable of sanity, is the Brahman to remain an exception to that sanity? Let us expect of our own country and of our own people, the highest and noblest and most progressive outlook that any people in the world might take. And in doing this, let us look to become Hindus, in a true sense, for the first time. For it is a question whether so grand a word ought to be borne by us unless we have first earned and approved our right to it. Ought not the name of our country and our faith to be to us as a sort of order of merit, a guerdon of loyal love, the token of accepted toil?

CO-OPERATION.

BOTH Hindus and Mohammedans have great need amongst themselves of such work as has been done amongst Christians, during the past century, by mutual association. No one would suggest that such forms of association should be deliberately imitated by Orientals amongst themselves. But a very different matter is the apprehension of the idea that is represented by the institution, and its re-expression in some other form. The impact of Western life and thought has shattered many of our own most precious methods of self-organization. The old village-community,—with its coherence, its moral order, its sense of purpose, and its openness to the highest thought and sacrifice,—has gone, and in its place we have the heap of disconnected fragments that goes in modern times by the name of a city.

Even the city, of the mediaeval epoch, had its own way of fulfilling the purposes of modern voluntary associations. The newcomer to Benares or Allahabad found himself immediately in his own quarter, surrounded by men from his own part of India, directly or indirectly connected with himself. In the outer apartments of their homes he met with friends, received assistance and advice, and was able to avail himself of local culture. This *para* of his own countrymen was to all intents and purposes his club, his home, his hospital. And it served all these ends far better than any modern society of the cities can possibly do. It was here that there grew up the organized communal opinion that resulted sooner or later in the extension of scope in required directions. For the communal organization in all provinces was generous, and free, and debonair, full of comradeship, rising in its richer members into princely liberality. It is the continuity of our social environment, moreover, that keeps us all on our own highest level in character and conduct. And this continuity was admirably provided for in the old city *paras*. The youth who came from the south in those days, was not open to the same temptations as now, from the dissipations of the city. And this for the good reason that the elders about him were men of his own district. The news of any lapses from decorum would assuredly travel back to the old people at home, and in the village of his birth his family would hang their heads for shame of him. It is not easy to estimate the moral restraint imposed by this series of facts.

While we remember this, however, we cannot fail to consider the contrast presented by modern developments. Let us think, for instance, of the crowds of poor Mohammedans who find their way into a city like Calcutta,—chiefly perhaps from Patna and Behar,—to act as syces and coachmen. The temptations of this particular life are notorious in all countries. Liquor-shops are banefully on the increase. The custom of congregating in one's own quarter is on the wane. Can it be wondered at that the life of the city proves utterly destructive to the happiness of many a simple country home?

And yet, though all this is but too true, we must not speak as if any people in the world could compare with our own people even here. Very often the poor man whose hold on life is so sadly impaired by the foreignness of his environment, is nevertheless struggling to live on one meal a day and send half of his tiny wages to his home. No one will ever know the whole history of the self-sacrifice of Indian servants in these days. The commonest of our countrymen are able to practise a control of hunger that in any other land would canonize them as martyrs.

We, and especially the student classes, who live in cities, would do well to consider the social problems that surround us. What can we do for the People? How can we strengthen the People to recover themselves? We are not called upon to create new forces of restitution. These, in abundance, are our heritage from our forefathers. But we are called upon to conserve, to use, to develop, and re-adjust to modern needs, the treasure of moral impulses and moralizing and co-ordinating institutions that is ours.

Let each of us ask himself, Where are the Sudras who have come from his father's village? Does one not know? Then how sadly one has failed in the duty of solidarity! Could one do anything to help them? Anything to share with them one's own privileges? One never knows, till one has tried, how many and how great those privileges are. What a revolution would be effected, and how quickly, in Indian ideas, if every student in the land took a vow each year to give twelve lessons to some person or group of persons who had no other means of education! Twelve lessons would not be a great tax on any one, yet how immensely helpful to the taught! The lessons might take the form of anything the teacher had to offer. Physical exercise would do, if that were all one could give. Reading and writing, or counting, would be good. But better than any of these would be talks about geography and history, or the interchange of simple scientific conceptions, or a training in the observation of the everyday facts about us.

Have we thought how the acquisition of a few ideas helps living, how an intellectual speculation, left to germinate in the mind, raises and deepens the days it colours? Knowledge is truly the bread of life. Let us hasten, with the best that is in us, to offer knowledge to all about us!

SECTARIANISM.

A GREAT deal is commonly said of the evil done by the existence of sects. It may be, however, that such statements take somewhat too much for granted; that they are made thoughtlessly; and that the whole question of the use and abuse of sects is worthy of careful consideration.

Undoubtedly the temper that splits hairs continually over minute differences of doctrine, that welcomes dispute, and divides societies on the slightest pretext, is mischievous and reprehensible. If sectarianism of this description be the necessary characteristic of sects, then the less we see of them the better. All sects must be regarded as an evil, and hardly anything could be an excuse for their creation. But is it necessary that the schismatic temper should be the one inevitable product of a sect?

It is not the desire to separate from others, but the desire of men to unite themselves together, round the banner of a common truth or ideal, that brings the sect into being. The sect is a *church*, and a church, to quote a time-honoured definition, is neither more nor less than "a company of faithful people." In this sense, we might almost call any body of persons associating themselves voluntarily for the purposes of some scholarly study, or learned idea, a sect, or church. In a sense, a gathering of the fellows of a medical society, or an Asiatic society, is a congregation. In a sense, since these bodies are made up of persons "faithful" to a certain idea, they are churches. And as soon as we say this, we realize that the sect is really an assertion of unity, not of difference; an association, not a separation; a brotherhood, not a schism.

But let us look at the religious body, the church gathered round some central idea of faith or conduct, the ecclesiastical church. Do sects of this kind play no large and generous purpose in the world, from which we may learn? Undoubtedly they do. In the first place, they form a confraternity, even, in a certain sense, a home. The struggling, poverty-stricken member has those about him who will aid, those whose communal interest lies in his well-being, those who will defend him from the sneers and oppression of the world without. This aspect of the sect may be seen in the Jewish, the Jain, and the Parsi communities.

The sect is also a school. The children of its members have a heritage in the idea, and their church is responsible for their education in it. They are born to a place in an army, and the ideals and discipline, as well as the solidarity, of soldiers, are theirs from the first moment of life.

The sect is an arena. Each member's life is plunged in the open, with the moral enthusiasm of all about him to be his guide and stay. The honour of the church demands the highest possible achievement of each one of its sons. She gives her hero parting salutation, and welcome on return. She treasures up every significant act of his life, and makes it available to those who live in his shadow. She provides a home and friends in the distant cities for the youth who fares forth to seek fortune and adventure. She is mother and friend and guardian, *guru* and generalissimo and banner, all in one. Is a sect altogether an evil?

Yet the final use of the sect is the transcending of sects. Its greatest sin is to deny the truth to those without. Every moment of our lives is Judgment-Day. Even at their culmination, when the part has been played with honour in the sight of all men, there is the question as to the spirit in which the whole shall be summed up. Shall we end by claiming the sole infallibility for ourselves? Or shall our final message be "Lo, this is the light that lighteth every man that cometh into the world"?

In India—the land from which the words just quoted surely emanated—there can be no doubt as to which of these is the true attitude. No one church has a monopoly of truth. No single shepherd is alone infallible. There is no final sect except Humanity, and that Humanity must include, as Buddha thought, all that lives and enshrines a soul.

The day may perhaps have gone by for the forming of sects, but not for taking their spirit and inspiring our own lives with it. As the church is a school, a home, a brotherhood, so let every village be, amongst us. As the sect is a great over-arching Motherhood, so be to us our country and our fellows. The religious band gathered round a common truth. But we are called together by the sacredness of our *place*. The ancient Aryan planted his altar, and lighted the sacred fire when he came to the spot that seemed to him most sacred. And so to us, every common hearth-place is the Vedic altar. The household, the village, the city, and the country, are they not so many different forth-shinings to the heart, of One Immensity of Motherhood? As Her children, born in the light of these Her shrines, are we not all one brotherhood in the closest of bonds?

THE SAMAJ.

A VISIT to a Christian church impresses one very powerfully with the organizing and co-operating instinct of the European races. Their religious thought, like that of the Jewish people from whom they derive it, often seems to us, in comparison with the rich background of Hinduism, poor, or even childish; but as to the beauty and impressiveness of their ceremonial and liturgical expression, there can be no dispute.

Nor do we class all Christian forms as equal in this respect. The old Latin Church, while much more historic, and much closer to Asiatic ritual, does not seem to us to compare, in the simple grandeur of its services, with the modern church of Anglican Protestantism. In the Roman Church, a great deal of the service is performed by a priest, on behalf of a silent kneeling congregation. This is parallel with the part played by the Brahman in our own services. The great stroke of genius, in which the European mind reaches its most distinctive manifestation, appears to have been the invention of Common Prayer. It was perhaps the Mohammedans who first thought of it,[1] and Europe had been saturated with the idea of Moham-

[1] Sister Nivedita, quoting Swami Vivekananda, was accustomed to attribute the institution of common prayer to Islam. This view overlooks its establishment in Jewish worship many centuries earlier.—EDITOR.

medan institutions, doubtless, throughout the whole period of the Crusades. Then again, one of the most powerful contributory causes of the Reformation itself had lain in the capture of Constantinople, in 1453 A.D., by the Ottoman Turks. This was an event which must, in the nature of things, have revived and deepened the European tradition of the Saracen and his ways. And who shall say what impression falls deepest into the mind of nation or individual, to germinate most powerfully?

Mean it what it may, it is certain that Christianity began by being an Asiatic idea, but ends, attaining its most distinctive characteristics, as European Protestantism; that common prayer—meaning the united prayer of the congregation, taking a definite part in the drama of worship—began with Islam, but ends in such places as the Anglican Church.

Hinduism possesses congregational worship in rudiment only. Hitherto, it has not greatly recognized anything beyond the priest and the single worshipping soul. Its view of the act of prayer is so much more intense than the European, that it would seem to it a confusion in terms to talk of such conceptions as democratic worship! And yet, for this worship by the individual soul, it offers the beaten paths of liturgy and ritual, written prayer and pre-determined act. In this, again, it provides us with the exact antithesis of Europe, where those sects who exalt the individual experience in matters spiritual become nonconformist, and discard all pre-determined expression and form.

Christianity produces very few *rishis* and great saints. Only at long intervals do we meet, in Europe, with a Francis, a Teresa, or a Joan. And we meet with them almost exclusively in the church of images and *Tapasyâ*, of *Sâdhanâ* and *Bhajana*. In spite of a Frances Ridley Havergal, and the American Shakers, in spite of Swedenborg amongst the *rishis*, and the Wesleys and Catherine Booth amongst the saints, Protestantism can hardly be said to have made up the full tale of numbers due from her as yet. The strength of Christianity, the strength of Europe, does not, in fact, lie in the exceptions it produces. Its strength lies in its average. It may be defective in greatness; it is remarkably well represented when it comes to a fair working level, of a somewhat crude type perhaps,—aggressive, very cocksure, extremely limited in ideas; but a success, when we consider how well it is held by the majority, how little, comparatively speaking, is the lapse below it. For this, Christianity has lopped off the heads of her tallest growths, that there might be none, either, hopelessly dwarfed. For this she makes her worship into a sort of literary and musical exercise, knowing well that we cannot constantly lend ourselves to the articulation of given ideas, without eventually becoming approximated to them in our own nature. For this, she has confined herself to the narrow ground of a scheme of salvation nineteen hundred years old. For this, she exalts service above *Jnânam*, and social utility above *Bhakti*—that she might create a strong, mutually-coherent, self-respecting average, and raise her multitudes to its level.

In matters of religion, a Hindu peasant seems like a cultivated man of the world beside what is often the childishness of a European man of letters. In matters of civic right, the humblest European will often regard as obvious and inevitable what is hidden from the Hindu leader and statesman.

But we are come to the age of the Interchange of Ideals. Humanity does not repeat her lessons. What is learnt in one province of her great kingdom she expects another to take and use. Undoubtedly the thought of the East is about to effect the conquest of the West. And the ideals of the West, in turn, are to play their part in the evolution of the East. This point of view has little in common with that of the missionary, for it means that *neither will displace the other*. Each will act as complementary only.

Hinduism will undoubtedly in the future develop a larger democratic element. She will begin to recognize the value of liturgical prayer. A new consideration will be felt amongst us for the education and training of the average man. Notions of service, ideals of action, will come in, to re-enforce our too exclusive admiration for the higher forms of realization. It is to be hoped that we shall never lose our regard for the segregation of the soul, as the path to God. But without losing this, we could well afford to emphasize the potentialities of the crowd. To a certain extent, these tendencies have already found exemplification in the Arya, Brahmo, and Prarthana Samajes. In Bengal, the Adi Brahmo Samaj, of the Maharshi Devendranath Tagore, represents to us much that the Lutheran and Anglican Churches represent in Christianity. It is Protestant, so to speak, yet liturgical; full of tradition, yet congregational. The Sadharan Brahmo Samaj, on the other hand, corresponds to the nonconforming sects in England. There is still in it, perhaps, a greater regard for inherited prayers and formulæ than amongst the iconoclasts of Europe. But this is not to be wondered at, in a religion so much more venerable than theirs as ours.

What we still want, nevertheless, is the taking up of these new features into modern orthodox Hinduism. If Hinduism is to become aggressive,—taking back its own perverted children, and holding its arms open to foreign converts,—it must also develop, so to speak, a democratic wing. The People must find a place and a united voice in its services. The procession must be made articulate in hymns and responses. There will be stated times of assembly,—and the temple steps may even become the pulpit, the place of exposition, and exhortation. All these changes will not displace the individual *puja*. None of us need fear the loss of religious treasures whose true value we are only now able to appreciate.

But these are the days of a great new outpouring of God upon our people, and the Mother-Church, ever responsive, will feel this and give it utterance, even as in the past she has reflected each phase of our national history. We shall abandon nothing, but add all things. For the sake of the many we shall learn to exalt action, to idealize work. But Hinduism will not, for all that, cease to be the school of the few, leading them to *Jnânam*, to *Bhakti*, to renunciation, and to *Mukti*.. Religion is not passive and static. It is dynamic, ever growing. This truth remains for us to prove.

THE PAST AND THE FUTURE.

SOME people strive to be truly Indian by looking back, and some aim at the same goal by looking forward. It is quite evident that we need both, yet that of the two the second is still the more important. We need the two, because the future must be created out of the strength of the past. None of us can be educated by rebuke alone. The teacher who really forms us, is he who sees better than we did ourselves what we really longed and strove for, how far our effort was right, and in what points we might make it still finer and better. He who interprets us to ourselves, and at the same time gives us hope, is the true educator.

In the same way a nation cannot be aided by contempt or abuse. The future cannot be founded on a past admitted to be a failure. He who attempts to do this will never understand his own defeat. Before we can teach, we must first worship the Divine that expresses itself through the taught. Service is really worship. Charity is worship. And even education is worship. Because I see in you the infinite *Atman*,—pure, free, irresistible and eternal,—I may help you to remove some of the barriers to Its free expression. If the whole of humanity were *not* in you, what would be the use of our efforts? They could bring forth no fruit.

It follows that the advance of communities, like that of individuals, depends in the first place upon a clear conception of the goal before them, and a reverent appreciation of the work they have done in the past towards that end. Hence there *must* be a certain element of conservatism in all great social upheavals.

But it would be better to be confined to the future than to be confined to the past! After all, whether we know it or not, we cannot help carrying a certain amount of our inherited strength with us. And we *must* be hewing out the path for the advance of others. It is this tendency to limitation, to refuse full freedom to others, that is apt to make the young so impatient of what they take to be blind reaction. But the fault is not in conservatism itself, as our youth themselves will one day come to see, but rather in its denial of freedom to advance. All religions are true, as Sri Ramakrishna taught us, and practically everything in them is true, save and except those points in which they declare other faiths to be false. Similarly, our conservatives are right enough, except when they say that the youngsters are wrong, and the youngsters are true, except when they fret against the back-looking elders.

Each has need to love and pray for the success of the other. Do we want to see India turned into a pale copy of America? God forbid! How precious, as a bulwark against our own impatience then, are these staunch old believers who hold the national treasure, and guard the national colour, against all innovation! But do we want to see India with her wings clipped, chained to the roosting-perch, unable to do or to be or to soar where she will? If not, let our love and benediction go everywhere with our wayward children, in their sublime assault upon the future. On, on, strong souls, with your experiments in progress, your fiery hopes, and your fearless forward march! We know the love that burns in your hearts for the village home, and the father and grandfather. Better, we hold, could the land do without us than without you! The time will yet come when you will return to the old home, tired of wandering, weary of the fight, and leaving your own children to man the breach you leave, will turn your hearts to the ancient wisdom, and seek the final release. How grateful will you then be to the grey heads that preserved the national home! No other refuge could have seemed so cool as this old house. No music could have been so sweet as these temple bells. It is for the future that the past lives on. The past has no *bhakta* to compare with that future!

RELIGION AND NATIONAL SUCCESS.

We cannot too strongly condemn the reckless nonsense that is sometimes talked amongst our countrymen to the effect that countries are rendered effete by their religion, that by reason of her religion India has fallen upon a period of decline, and that because she has no religion Japan is a success.

The difficulty in dealing with this tangle of untruths is to know where to begin. Shall we first attack our friends' notion of what is religion? Or would it be wiser first to notice their idea of what constitutes the decline and success of countries? Some of us would indignantly reject the assumption that Japan is a success, preferring to maintain that precisely because she has no religion, in half a century she will be outstripped and forgotten.

Again, some of us would decline to admit that India is in a state of decay, being prepared to hold against all-comers the contrary opinion that she stands on the threshold of a great future, and feels coursing within her veins the blood of youth.

But these are matters in which our personal temperament and experience will largely determine our view. Hence, argument is more or less useless about them. The only demonstration that can be really successful will be that of the new heaven and the new earth, rising up about us, and the evidence of our senses themselves as to the truth. That argument will *not* be created by those who despair and talk of senile exhaustion!

The main point to be considered is what our friends are pleased to mean by religion. Perhaps, when this is well defined, we shall see that if India is not dead to-day, she owes her survival to the fact of her religion. Religion in this sense is not superstition, it is not fear, or mythology, or the practice of penances. It is living thought and belief, with their reaction in *character*.

Hinduism is not in this sense an idolatry of the fugitive. Success is as fleeting in the lives of nations as is defeat. Hinduism is no gospel of success. It does not even profess to hold out any short cut there. To do this is the domain of magic. Our religion is something better than a series of magical formulæ. If Hinduism were the gospel of success, it would belong only to one-half of experience.

When we are true to the faith that is in us, we become the witness, looking on at the spectacle of victory and of defeat. Seeking for triumph to the utmost of our power, we are not therefore enslaved by it. Striving with all our might to reverse our defeat, we are nevertheless not bowed down by it. In conquering as in being conquered, we stand serene, in the power of religion, conscious of a sovereign self-restraint within that yields to none of the circumstances of life, whether these be good or ill. Are we indeed jealous of those whose whole good is in the world about them? Do we not know that in the pairs of opposites there is oscillation, that good is followed by ill, fame by ignominy, brilliant success by blackness of disaster?

Religion is the permanent element, the accumulation of human thought and character in the midst of the ebb and flow of circumstance. This building up of the corporate personality is closely associated with the maintenance of native religious ideas. Who shall restore ancient Egypt, or Mesopotamia, Chaldæa or Assyria? None, for the things that made them individuals have disappeared for ever. Even a language can only persist round some central expression of a people's genius. We must not be misled by the brilliance of a moment. Where is Rome? Where is Portugal? Where is Spain? A few centuries are to the spirit of history only as an hour in the life of an ordinary man. Nations are not made or unmade by the flight of time, but by the steadiness and patience with which they hold, or do not hold, to the trust that it is theirs to carry through the ages. A moment of brilliant commercial exploitation does not constitute historic success, unless there are forces at work to maintain intact the personality of the victor. Nor can that commercial success itself endure, apart from character and integrity in those who have achieved it. Our religion teaches us that this world is not real. It is impossible for one who sincerely holds this, to barter the life of mind and conscience for external ease and comfort. Yet this preference of conscience above the interest of the moment is the master-quality in attaining the inheritance even of the earth itself.

THE SPIRIT OF RENUNCIATION.

AMONGST fallacies which are characteristic of special states of society there is in modern times none which is more common than the question, "Does it pay?" The remark ought always to be answered by a counter-question. "Pay whom?" And until this is clearly and fully replied to, no further answer should be given.

It will generally be found that the reference is to the individual. Is a given course of conduct likely to benefit that individual who engages in it, within a certain relatively short period? If so, that conduct is advisable, but if otherwise, then not.

Now this would be all very well, if a sufficiently large meaning could be given to the idea of the individual, or to the notion of what his benefit involved. Unfortunately, however, the class of mind to which the argument appeals strongly and clearly is not one which is capable of giving a larger significance to anything. If we are contemplating a course of vice it is a fair argument to ask "Does it pay?" because vice or sin of any kind is always in the long run detrimental to the best interests not only of the individual but also of the society.

Every advance in human knowledge, every invention, every achievement, almost without exception, throughout the history of Humanity, has been gained by those who had abandoned the idea of profit for themselves, and who were contented to labour for the profit of mankind. We are too apt, in India, to regard this as an ideal proper to the *sannyasin* only. We have to learn to-day that there must be no society without its *sannyasins*, and that many social applications have yet to be found for *Sannyas*.

As a matter of fact, curiously few undertakings are capable in all their stages of paying the individual. There is nothing which is more necessary socially than education. Yet is it not notorious that only in exceptional states of society can the educator be adequately paid? Why do the religious orders of the Roman Catholic Church carry so much of the educational burden in countries that are not Roman Catholic? Only because the individual worker contributes his service, as far as his community is concerned, free of charge. And thus his community triumphs. The training of the men whom it attracts ensures its prestige, their unselfishness its victory. This is the case with education to-day. But the same happened in Central Europe in earlier ages, with regard to other equally important activities. Thus J. R. Green says of the Begging Friars, or *sannyasins*, who came to England in the year 1224 A.D. :—

"The work of the Friars was physical as well as moral. The rapid progress of population within the boroughs had outstripped the sanitary regulations of the middle ages, and fever or plague or the more terrible scourge of leprosy festered in the wretched hovels of the suburbs. It was to haunts such as these that Francis had pointed his disciples, and the Grey

Brethren at once fixed themselves in the meanest and poorest quarters of each town. Their first work lay in the noisome lazar-houses, it was amongst the lepers that they commonly chose the site of their homes. At London they settled in the shambles of Newgate; at Oxford they made their way to the swampy ground between its walls and the streams of Thames. Huts of mud and timber, as mean as the huts around them, rose within the rough fence and ditch that bounded the friary."

All this was in the thirteenth century. But at the end of the eleventh, there had already arisen in Europe an austere order of monks, known as the Cistercians, who spread themselves over the moors and forests of France and the Rhine-countries; built abbeys and cathedrals; began agriculture on a large scale; drained the swamps, and cleared the common-lands. It was these Cistercians who afterwards sent out from their English mother-houses daughter-communities to settle in Norway, and these it was who alone in that country were able to practise building in stone, and who taught Roman letters, and enabled the people to write down their national epics.

Thus even the West—notwithstanding her present loud assertions of self-interest and quick profit as valid motives of action—even the West is built up on unpaid labour, on labour whose hire the labourers remitted and allowed to accumulate in the interests of the commonwealth. In fact it is only after an activity has been thoroughly institutionalized, and made common and standard, that it can expect to command a market rate of wages, so to speak. But before it can be institutionalized, it has to be explored and experimented on by some one or many of the more heroic pioneer-souls, in the cause of the community or of the race.

Even the English in India, with all their corporate selfishness, trace back their rights, as we remember, to a certain physician who would accept from a Mogul sovereign no personal reward but a factory-concession for the merchants, his fellow-countrymen. There is no need to fear a movement that has no *Sannyas* at its command. We shall find, however, that the counterpart of such *Sannyas* is always a strong and ever-present conception of the community. It was because Dr. Hamilton was so well aware of the needs of the company of merchants, and because he felt himself so strongly to be one of them, that he was able to be unselfish on their behalf. And therefore the true birth of an era takes place with a rise of a new idea of social combination.

There is no question as to what will eventually be done in India in the name of Nationality. Let only the thought of the nation be vivid enough, and it will carry all the necessary sacrifice in its train. And such sacrifice, for the nation, for the city, for the commonweal, is the school for that loftier, more remote sacrifice, which Hinduism knows as *Vairagyam*. He who has practised the civic *Sannyas* is best prepared for the national service. And he who has been chastened and purified in the national unselfishness is the most ready for that last and highest renunciation which reacts in life as *Jnânam*, or *Bhakti*, or *Karma-Yoga*.

But through what a strange series of *Sâdhanâs* is

this emancipation to be brought about! Children will need to renounce personal ambition, and parents to make the deeper renunciation of ambition for their children. And yet these *tyâgis* of the new time will wear no *gerrua*. Seated in an office or ruling over a factory; enrolling his fellows in unions, or studying with every nerve and muscle the organization of labour on a large scale; giving himself to education, or even, it may be, ruling faithfully and devotedly over a household of his own, not in the name of its limited interests, but against its interests, on behalf of the Indian people, such will be the *gerrua*-clad of the new order.

"He who knows neither fear nor desire," says the Gita, "is the true monk." Not the *sannyasin*-clad, but the *sannyasin*-hearted. He who has neither fear for himself nor hope for himself. He who could see his own family starve, if need were, in the communal cause. He who is contented to fail, if only out of his failure others may sometime in the future succeed. He who has no home outside his work, no possession save a selfless motive, no hope save that which his own blood shall enable his fellows to realize. These are the men who are to be found in every class of students to-day. And we dare to say to them, and to their neighbours and parents: Trust these high hopes that surge up within you! Risk all on your great hopes! Believe in yourselves, and in those who shall succeed you! So forward. Do what you see, and trust Mother for the next step. For verily it is of your hearts and your minds, of your life and your work that the New India which is to come shall yet be made. And blessed are ye who have not seen and yet can believe!

THE SACRED AND THE SECULAR.

INDIA alone, amongst all the countries of the earth, has had the boldness that could abolish the mental barriers between sacred and secular, high and low. India alone, having thought out the great philosophy of Advaita, has had the imagination to command Man to become the Witness, to declare life to be only play. It is a lofty task, to be worthy of the deeds and the dreams of our ancestors. Yet if we walk not their road, how shall we call others there?

"And the Lord said, 'Simon, Simon, Satan hath desired to have thee, that he may sift thee as wheat!'" These sombre words are recorded in the Christian Gospel of St. Luke, as spoken by Christ, only an hour or two before He was betrayed to His enemies. Such is the strength of the Avatar, that when the whole world has conspired to put Him on His trial, to hypnotize Him into a belief in His own weakness and forlornness, He is only conscious the while of putting the world on its trial, and sifting it as wheat. He is the one steady point in the great matrix of humanity, quivering, sifting, and oscillating in all directions. He is the point of inversion of all the feebleness and weakness of the common mind.

And from this point of view, the occurrence of the

Divine Man is a logical necessity. Without Him, as the spiritual pole, the tendency to co-ordinate our wandering impulses in the fixed outlines of character would be impossible. Even the meanest and poorest of us, inasmuch as we are man at all, are witnesses to Him, since all our efforts culminate in Him. Even the least of our strivings relates us to His vast achievement, and to that alone. Seen in this light, how true it is that we should pray for more strength, and not for lighter burdens! It is strength we want, not calm. Calm is only a result. It can be cultivated by practice. But if we have strength as the root, then calm and peace and steadfastness cannot fail to be its flower.

The ego that is identified with the body has its gaze entirely on one set of phenomena. It sees itself attacked, condemned, suffering, and scorned. The ego that identifies itself with Brahman is directly aware of none of these things. Afar off, it may be the witness of them. But its gaze is fixed on the opposite whorl of movement, that of spiritual intensity, and to it, it appears that the world is being put to the test. He who knows Himself to be One with the whole universe, how should He think of loneliness, how dream of passivity? He knows Himself as the persecutor, as well as the persecuted, and both alike as "the Mother's Play." Unbroken *Sachchidânanda* is His consciousness, unflawed bliss is in His bearing. And in Him meet the hopes and longings of us all.

There is one form of realization which can be developed in the *thakur-ghar*, and quite another in the rough-and-tumble of the world. Both, let us remember, are realization. Both are paths hewn through the mind to the knowledge of Brahman. Only the science of the Avatar can help us, even in the life of street and market-place. In *Sachchidânanda* culminate all joys and all knowledge, even the knowledge and the joy of earth.

QUIT YE LIKE MEN!

ALL is in the mind. Nothing outside us has any power save what we give it. However imposing the external world may seem, it is in reality only the toy of mind. It is but a feeble expression of what has first been *thought.* "*All that we are is the result of what we have thought,*" says Buddha; "it is founded on our thoughts; it is made up of our thoughts."

It is for this reason that education is so much the most important concern of life. The mind must be kept in a condition to work. It must be held at the command of the will, from its lowest up to the highest possible activity. It must be made competent to envisage any problem, and answer it in a fashion not inadequate. A people can afford to eat poorer food, and less of it, than was their custom. They cannot afford to let the mind grow dim. They cannot afford to part with education.

In this, the question is not of the particular subject through which we receive education. The question is of the mind itself, of the education behind the subject. Whatever the form of the drill, we must keep up our intellectual potentiality. There are two factors in this question,—one is that of the particular tool or weapon, the other that of the mental muscle, the training of the limb that gives the grip. It is well, doubtless, to be familiar with the sword: it is better far to have power of arm. Whether by Sanskrit or by technology, by mathematics or by poetry, by English or by classic, does not matter. These are but the toys through which the power is won. What we want is the power itself, power of concentration, power of thought.

India has been strangely fortunate in the production of this power. This is what the practice of concentration means. This is what *samâdhi*, if we could reach it, would mean. This is what prayers and *pujas* and *japams* all aim at,—the power of controlling the mind, carried to its highest point. A people must ultimately measure itself against others, not in terms of force, but in terms of mind. Their superiority may be invisible, may be held in solution, as it were, waiting for the favourable moment to form the dense precipitate. But let them only practise. Let them only never relax. And the potentiality of self-recovery will not pass away.

Yet we should not allow our superiority to be invisible, or held in suspension. We should be fully equal to its assertion. It will be remembered how little Sri Ramakrishna admired the cobra who abandoned not only biting, but also even hissing. A whole community that knew how to hiss, would mean a community that never required to bite. "Peace on earth" is only, really, to be attained by this means! How keen and clear was the intellect that saw this, and laid it down as a great human ideal! How masterly was that other mind that penetrated all our controversies and summed up all our perplexities in the one pronouncement, "Quit ye like men!"

And how are we to quit us like men? By never

sitting down short of the goal. By aspiring to the front on the field of battle, and the back in the durbar. By struggle, struggle, struggle, within and without. Above all, by every form of self-mastery and self-direction. There is no tool that we must not try to wield, no weapon that we can be content to leave to others. In every field we must enter into the world-struggle. And we must aim at defeating every competitor. The New Learning is ours, no less than other men's. The search for truth is ours, and we are as well equipped for it as any. Civic integrity is ours. We have only to demonstrate it. Honour is ours. We may have to carry it into places new and strange. The communal consciousness, the corporate individuality, all are ours, though we have to express them in unknown ways. Public spirit and self-sacrifice, we are capable of these.

But to realize the ideal that these words call up before us, we must struggle for education of all kinds, as captives for air, as the famine-stricken for food. We must capture for ourselves the means of a fair struggle, and then, turn on us all the whiteness of your searchlights, oh ye tests of modern progress! Ye shall not find the children of India shrink from the fierceness of your glow!

SINCERITY.

LET us, in our own lives, and in the training of our children, try to get back to the fundamental virtues. None can ask us for success. Any may demand of us truth, simplicity, purity, courage. All these are only so many different faces, as it were, of one central perseverance in virtue, one nuclear sincerity, which makes the whole life of a man into a patient following of a thread, an idea, which he sees within his mind.

This patience, this steadfastness, this sincerity, is *Dharma*—the substance, the self-ness, of things and of men. *Dharma* makes us the toys of the great world-forces. Do we desire to be other? It makes us as dead leaves borne onwards by the furious tempests of the conscience. Is there a higher lot? Instruments of ideas, used, not using; slaves of the gods, scourged along all the thorny roads of life; resting not, fearing not, embracing ecstasy at the heart of despair.

Sincerity is what we want. Sincerity is the key and foundation of all realizations. Sincerity is the simplest of all the great qualities, and of them all, it goes the farthest. Sincerity and the heart fixed steadfastly on the Unseen—it is the whole of victory. Truth, purity, courage,—can their opposites exist in him who is sincere? Are they not all forms of that one clear-sightedness? The man who step by step proceeds towards his own soul's quest, conscious of that and that alone, is there any lie, cowardice, or grossness that can tempt him?

The opposite of sincerity is ostentation, hypocrisy, love of show. To seek constantly for advertisement, to talk big, to ask for results instead of methods, this is to undermine sincerity, to build up stuff of failure instead of triumph. It is this, of which we must seek to root out even the incipient impulse. It is this over which we must strive to help our children. It is this that we must learn to avoid with passionate horror. By reserve, by modesty, by labour to make the deed greater than the word, we must deny and punish that thing in us that cries out for self-assertion, for cheap praise, and easy notoriety.

Everything in the modern world tends to foster the habit of loud talk. We have travelled far away from the quiet dignity and simple pride of our forefathers. Their freedom from self-consciousness is what we want. But it is to be got in one way, and one alone. We must do as they did, take ideals and thoughts that are greater than ourselves and set them before us, till our life's end, as the goals of the soul. Only when we are merged in the flood-tide that is God, can we in very truth forget the reflection in the mirror that is called the Ego. And the flood-tide of God takes many names, some amongst them being strangely familiar in their spelling. Let us live for anything, so only it be great enough to teach us forgetfulness of self! Forgetfulness of self is in itself the finding of God.

FACING DEATH.

THE worshipper of God as a Providence does undoubtedly gain something from his worship in courage; since every man believes instinctively that God is *with him*, whomsoever He might be against. Yet nothing can wipe out from Providence-worships the stain of *using* God, of subordinating Him to the petty interests of Self.

The belief in Destiny has its dangers, also. For we sink so easily into the assumption that Destiny alone is active, while we regard ourselves as passive. Yet the truth in fact is that we are active and dominant, and Destiny at the most is passive. "Kismet!" cries the Arab soldier, as he speeds forward in the charge, or rushes madly into the breach. No soldier, for an immediate victory, like this. But "Kismet!" he mutters again, solemnly, as the return fire forces his first rush backwards,—and that very belief in Destiny that made him a moment ago the fiercest soldier in the world, makes him now the most difficult to rally.

Different from either of these is the courage born of Mother-worship in Hinduism. Here, the embrace is death, the reward is pain, the courage is rapture—*All*, not the good alone, is Her touch on the brow—*All*, not simply the beneficent, is Her will for Her child. "Where shall I look," he cries, "that Thou art not?

If I take the wings of the morning and fly unto the uttermost parts of the sea, lo, Thou art there! If I go down into Hell, Thou art there also!"

The worship of the Mother is in truth the Vedanta of the hero. She is the whole, the Primal Force, the Infinite Power, the Adi-Sakti. To become one-d with That Power is to reach *samâdhi.* It is by blotting out self, by annihilating personality, that we may enter that vision. "When desire is gone, and all the cords of the heart are broken, *then*," says the Veda, "a man attains to immortality."

We do not naturally love that whose strength is too great for us. One who had been left alone for a few minutes in a cavern beside Niagara, told of a passion of hatred that overwhelmed her as she looked. It was the active form of physical fear. We should feel the same hatred, perhaps, for the midnight universe that looks now to us so brilliantly beautiful, were we free to move along the paths of the stars, and come face to face with foreign suns. Our emotions are, for the most part, the result of an immediate and subconscious measurement of ourselves and our relations to that by which we are confronted. To few indeed has it been given to know "the joy of the witness." To fewer still, the last and highest rapture of the union, once for all, with the Mother.

Those who would reach this must worship Death. Drinking the cup of suffering to the dregs, again and again they will hold it out, empty, for more. To the strong, no going back; to the resolute, no disillusionment. The disillusionments of which we read in poetry are not signs of strength. They are sudden reactions of self-consciousness and egoism, at unexpected movements. The hero, with his irresistible energy, and his unflinching gaiety, does not know whether that which meets him is pleasant or sad. He goes through it, and demands more. He treads on a sword as it were on air. He has passed beyond self.

"Sri Ramakrishna," said the Swami Vivekananda, "never thought of being humble. But he had long ago forgotten that Ramakrishna ever existed." This is the energy, and this the courage, of the Mother-worshipper. He who has realized the Infinite, of what shall he be afraid? Death is contained within him. How then shall he fear death? In what shall he think pain different from pleasure? He has broken the great illusion. How shall it be of avail against him? Says George Eliot—

> "Strong souls live like fire-hearted suns,
> To spend their strength in farthest action.
> Breathe more free in mighty anguish
> Than in trivial ease."

And the words ring true. For such is strength. And such are the heroes who are born of Mother.

LUXURY AND MANHOOD.

NOTHING is a greater test of education than the noble employment of leisure and means. It is not nearly so much by our performance of duties, as by our selection of interests, that our character is revealed. This is why an age of luxury is apt to act so disastrously on the richer classes. The man who would have been a gentleman and a man of honour, under steady toil, becomes a mere animal, and sometimes not even a sane or healthy animal, when his whole life is turned into play. When the standards of luxury, however, by which we are invaded, are imported and extraneous to our civilization, their danger to the conscience is increased a hundred-fold. The moral sense of Europe itself can hardly stand against the intensification of waste which has come in with the motor car. How then were Indian princes to resist the sudden incursion of alcohol, sport, and the acquaintance with Western methods of gambling,—all these being bestowed upon them, moreover, by individuals who remained more or less unaffected themselves by any of the deeper ethical idealisms of their own world?

Yet it is precisely by the types of freedom which it develops that a system is to be judged. There are many different ways of arriving at a given end. A man may arrive at personal cleanliness, refinement, and honour, by methods Hindu, Mohammedan, or European. But whatever be the road he takes, he must, in the end, prove himself a gentleman, or the method of his training stands condemned. Betting, smoke-soddenness, and intoxication, are not the marks of a man of good breeding in Europe, any more than in the East. And even when they do occur, in their native habitat, they usually tend to be somewhat corrected, in their manifestation, by the social habits of their proper environment. A certain alertness of manner must be maintained in Western circles, if a man is not to be set down by his associates as an effeminate fool. Personal diffidence and an instinctive courtesy to, and responsibility for the protection of, women and the weak, are demanded of every one. Spareness of form and hardness of muscles, together with the readiness to shoulder physical hardships with enjoyment, are absolute essentials of the gentleman. Thus the caste-ideal tends in some measure to correct caste-vice. But the adhesion of the individual to the ideal is often automatic and only half-conscious. The things that are apt to pass on energetically to a royal Indian pupil are the vices, instead of the virtues, of his class.

Corresponding truths hold, in various degrees, of all the ranks affected by Western habits. We are only too likely to catch the contagion of luxury instead of that of ideals. The Englishman's society allows him to drink tea in the morning, but requires that when he travels away from railways, he shall either walk or ride. Our danger is, lest we indulge in the tea but continue to have ourselves wheeled in rickshaws, or carried in chairs and dandies. The Englishman eats well, but he also works well ; he never refers to his health in public ; he masters the use of a weapon, and goes through life (if he be true to his ideals) at the price of his own power to defend himself, "like a man." It is much easier for the foreigner to catch his habit of eating chicken than his strenuous suppression of the letter "I" and arduous avoidance of degrading ease. It is much easier to emulate his privileges than his manliness and notions of personal dignity.

Forewarned, however, is forearmed. Few of us realize the power, in saving us from moral danger, of clear thought. Our own ideals are our best armour. Let us keep our minds clear as to what constitutes glory of manhood, and glory of womanhood. Doing this, each increment of ease and wealth becomes fresh material for sacrifice to some noble object.

STRENGTH.

RENUNCIATION is always of the lower, for the sake of the higher. It is never of the higher, in order to possess the lower. Renunciation is of the easy, in favour of the difficult,—of the superficial, to reach the profound. It proposes new duties: it never bestows ease.

Sri Ramakrishna's wonderful story of the penitent cobra contains in a sentence the whole doctrine of personal dignity and power. "Raise the hood, but don't bite!"—how many occasions are there in life, when this gives us the key of the situation! With how many persons do we maintain excellent relations merely because they know that at a moment's notice, on the slightest infringement of our relative positions, our sweetness would leave us, and we should become threatening in attitude, menacing, hostile! The cobra would, in other words, have lifted his hood.

But we must not make the mistake of supposing that every act of fretfulness or irritation is such a lifting of the hood. In the cobra we find a developed power of anger, a trained power to use the most formidable weapons of offence in the world, an instant perception of the moment's need, and, above all, *every one of these held in conscious restraint.* It is the power behind him that makes the serpent so formidable. It is no use for fools or cowards to talk of lifting the hood! It follows that there were years of growth behind the penitence of our hero, during which his sole duty was to become the cobra. *Having gained his power*, true strength was shown by controlling it. It is the duty of every man to be the cobra. Ours is no gospel of weaklings! We ought so to live that in our presence can be wrought no wrong. Even biting may be needful, when the power of the cobra is not understood, but the hurt dealt should always be by way of warning, never an act of vengeance. Relatively to our consciousness of strength, it must only be the lifting of the hood.

All these truths are easily seen in the punishment of a child. What should we think of the parent whose whole soul went into the chastisement of his son? It is evident here that there must be a certain detachment, a certain aloofness from our own action, if the punishment is ever to be effective. Punishment given in anger rouses nothing but the contempt of a culprit. Punishment gravely and sorrowfully dealt out, by one who is conscious the while of the ideal that has been outraged, converts while it pains.

Force is only well used by the man who has an idea beyond force. Force is meant to be used, not to carry us away on its flood. It represents the horses, well-reined-in by the successful driver. Restraint is the highest expression of strength. But strength must first be present, to be restrained. No one respects the man without courage: and no one respects the blind human brute, whose actions are at the mercy of his own impulses of rage. Ours is the religion of strength. To be strong is, to our thinking, the first duty of man. So to live that our mere presence enforces righteousness, and protects weakness, is no mean form of personal achievement.

TRUE AMBITION.

EVERY man's estimate of himself is a focussing-point for his estimate of the society to which he belongs. Is there anything that makes proud like the consciousness of family? Is there anything that makes sensitive like pride of race? That man who gives high respect to others is the same who demands the finest courtesy for himself. By the freedom we constantly assert, we appraise the freedom of our blood in the eyes of the whole world.

The pride of birth has been cultivated in India, for thousands of years, as a social and national safeguard. Like other forms of pride, it is a virtue when it is positive, and a vice only when it denies the right of equal pride to others. The vanity that cuts us off from the community, telling us that we are better than they, is petty and vulgar, and while it humiliates those whom we would insult, it only makes a laughing-stock of ourselves in the eyes of all who are competent to judge. However celebrated our family, it is hardly possible to be of such exalted birth that there is not anyone else in any single respect still more exalted. Our joy therefore can at best be but relative, till it may dawn upon us that the greatest distinction lies in simplicity, and that privilege or monopoly is, after all, conterminous with meanness.

Pride of birth, in fact, like other forms of *Karma*, should be regarded as an opportunity, a responsibility, a trust. The higher my position, the more difficult and arduous my duty. The purer my inheritance, the greater my powers of endurance. If we could but see truly, we should know that to be a man is to be nobly born, and our merit remains for us to prove. All things are possible to all men, for equally are the expressions of the Infinite, the Pure, the All-knowing, the Free. Man may make distinctions between man and man. But God makes none. He opens to each one of us the franchise of struggle, and leaves it to us to make our own place.

Oh for lofty ambitions! What shall we do with our lives? Let us swear to eliminate self. Walking any path, doing any task, let us pursue the ideal for its own sake, the ideal to the utmost, the ideal to the end. Whatever we do, let us do it with our might. Spurning ease, forsaking gain, renouncing self, let us snatch the highest achievement that offers itself, at any cost, and cease not from struggle till it is in our hands. This is what was meant by the ancient reformers, when they said "he who attains to God is the true Brahman." Birth was but a preliminary condition, and that not essential; it could never be substituted for the end itself.

Every study has its own problems. The Modern Learning carries its own questions. The Brahman of to-day ought to enter into these. He ought to share the modern curiosity. The whole of education is complete if we once waken in a child a thirst for knowledge. Can we not waken a like thirst in ourselves? Are flying-machines and motors to receive no elaboration from the Indian mind? Is that mind not equal to such tasks? Then is it inferior to the European? If we claim equality, on us lies the responsibility of proving the claim. Let us do away with trumpery ambitions! Let us learn in order to teach the world, in order to win truth for Humanity, not in order to strut in borrowed plumes before a village crowd. Let us be severe with ourselves. Let us know, on the subject we take up, all that there is to be known. Let us read great books. Let us make perfect collections. No difficulty should daunt us. Fate offers obstacles that man may overcome. Thus he becomes the nursling of the gods, gifted with divine strength, and seats himself amidst the immortals.

In great struggles all men are equal. Anyone may enter these lists. The prize is to the winner, high or low, man or woman. But no man can rise alone. Collective effort is essential. He who mounts far must have twenty behind him, close upon his heels. Our learning is not all our own. We gain it through others, as well as by our own effort. Alone, we could not cover the necessary ground. Our society sets us a high standard, and shining there, we succeed before the world. Thus each one is aided by the victory of any other, and the glory of one is the glory of all.

Thought, thought, we want clear thought! And for clear thought, labour is necessary, knowledge is necessary, struggle is necessary. Clear thought and rightly-placed affection are essential conditions of victory in any field. The nation that is true to itself and its age will give birth to millions of great men, for the inflowing of the Divine Spirit is without limit, and the greatness of one is the greatness of all.

CHARACTER.

CHARACTER is latency. A man's very being is the record of his whole past. This is the secret of the profound significance of history. The future cannot be different from the past, any more than a man's body can be inherited from the ancestors of another.

But the future is not born of some portion only of the past. It is born and created and conditioned by the whole. This is what is really meant by the doctrine of *Karma*. The East, with its belief in re-incarnation, has a wonderful instrument for the understanding and discrimination of life. It catches shades and tints of personality that others could not distinguish. In what the man is, it can read what he aspired to. In what he unconsciously does, it can see the past. The throne may often fall to the lot of one who was used to be a slave. But we may be sure that for deeply penetrating sight the monarch's robes cannot conceal the lash-marks on his back. The serf may many times have been an emperor. The keen observer will not fail to note the ring of command in his voice, the eye of decision in a crisis, the flush of pride rising hot under insult.

The whole of a man is in his every act, however difficult to the world be the reading of the script. Noble longing is never vain. Lofty resolve is never wasted. As the act is expression of the man, so is the life the expression of the character. And so is the character the key to the life. The only sequences that never fail are the spiritual truths. "All that we are is the result of what we have thought." Water rises to its own level, say the engineers, and what is true of water is as true of the mind of man. One step gained in mastery finds a million applications. As high as we have climbed on this mountain, so high shall we attain, without rest or hindrance, on every height whereon our feet shall be set. The man ruling an empire may be doing nothing more in reality than re-acting the part he played in the games of his childhood. A Wellington, in his babyhood, fights all the battles of the future with his wooden soldiers. Even so one who has once found the secret of unity will never rest, in any birth, till he has reached once more, through the material he finds about him there, as deep a view.

How marvellous are the potentialities of humanity! There is no man so mean or servile but hides within himself the possibility of the Infinite. The ultimate fact in the world is man, not power: the ultimate fact in man is God. Therefore let all men believe in themselves. To all men let us say—Be strong. Quit ye like men. Work out that which worketh in you. Believe in yourselves. For he that asketh, receiveth; he that seeketh findeth, and to him that knocketh, it *shall* be opened. The whole past is in every man of us. At any moment may the Supreme Light shine through me. At any moment may my personal become the hand, the lips, of That Impersonal. Why then should I be weak, either in taking or in losing? Am I not the Infinite Itself? Of whom and of what should I be afraid? Henceforth do I cast aside pleading and prayer. Henceforth do I throw away all hope, all fear, all desire, all shame. Contented am I to be a man, and that alone. For I know that if I be not that, verily even the jewels of the king and robes of state shall not hide my shame, nor the rags of the beggar detract from the glory of my manhood, if I have it.

DISCRIMINATION.

THERE is a vast difference between the human being who lives his life like a mouse or a mole—from moment to moment, and sensation to sensation,—and the man who lives for an idea. Even a mistaken idea is infinitely higher than the life of the senses. Even the poorest of those who strive to walk in the footsteps of the saints is higher than the man, however grandiose his expression, however demonic his energy, whose life is limited to self, with its interests and pleasures. We must never allow mere size to impose upon us. Discrimination is the glow of spirituality upon each of the virtues. Without discrimination, man is no better than an animal, whatever the form that his animal comforts may take.

Youth admires careless and lavish giving. It thinks the man who sometimes refuses a gift, for a reason he will not tell, neither so great nor so generous as he who empties his pockets at the first chance call. The Gita, on the contrary, tells us that ideal charity is rightly timed and placed, and offered only to the proper person. It is evident that the gift, given with discrimination, is higher than the mere largesse, which never looks at the recipient, or foresees any one of its own effects.

In the same way, it is the level of our general discrimination, between mind and flesh, idea and sense, that determines, on the large scale, our rank as human beings. The Bible tells how a certain king made a golden image of himself and set it up for all the world to worship. And that same monarch, a little later, under the spell of mania, went out into the fields to eat grass with the cattle! The dazzling idealism of self covered the grossest animality. It was the same man who one day propounded a new religion, and the next crawled on all-fours! The poorest and lowest who is sincerely striving for unselfishness, for self-control, and to give love, is greater than this. That is why the real helpers of mankind have been unable to preach anything less than this ultimate truth. The difference between man and man lies, not in possessions, or in the positions they have achieved, or in the power they wield, but in the degree of their self-control, and in that alone.

"By any means *catching hold of things*," said Sri Ramakrishna, "make your way out of the world." Let us not forget this "catching hold." No religious man ought to think his behaviour in the world a matter of no consequence. Religion is not confined to *Sâdhanâs*. *Tapasyâ* is not a matter of the *thakur-ghar* alone. Every great idea that presents itself in the secular sphere is a form of God calling for our worship. Shall we range ourselves with it, or against it? The answer makes no difference to God, no difference to the truth, but it constitutes a judgment day of the soul. It makes all the difference in the world to us. Every day, every act, every question that arises, is a judgment day. Life is one long test.

To each little act we bring the whole weight of our character. Each act leaves us either stronger or weaker. It adds to or takes from our ultimate worth. Spirituality does not arise by accident. Only in a temple long and carefully builded of well-hewn blocks, can the image of universal and eternal truth be placed. Only where truth has been sought in all things, can the lamp of Truth be lighted in the soul. Discrimination in every act of life makes for that last discrimination that is eternal bliss.

FITNESS.

THE Eternal Faith holds up as the Ideal that there shall be *fitness* in every thought and action, over and above the *goodness* that it expresses. In this way, amongst others, the Mother Church labours to impress upon us the necessity of thought, of knowledge, of intellectual maturity. Learning is as necessary to the Hindu faith as prayer—the only religious doctrine in the world that has no quarrel with truth, wherever it may be found, or wherever it may be. Think of it! Other religions may *tolerate* science, or persons within their fold may see that they owe a duty to themselves or to knowledge; but Hinduism *requires* it. Like the clear welling-forth of water from a deep spring should be the thought of great Hindu thinkers.

Alas, the very absence of resistance is apt to take away the force of activity! Europe is full of great scholars. How many have we? Yet look at the difference! In Europe the whole world, and especially the priesthood, barked and yelped at the heels of Charles Darwin for twenty years. Even to-day, one will hear a sneer from the pulpit levelled against Buckle or Lecky. Every priest feels secretly that there is an antagonism between his cause and that of the unfettered historian or critic: in India, such fears are referred to as "sectarianism." But the very attack on truth is a war-cry calling the young to rally to its defence. We all know the story of the captain sent with his thirty-three men, to deliver terms of surrender to Hasan and Hussain, who, his message done, ranged himself and his followers under their banner, though for them the result could be nothing but death. In all ages it is the same. Truth is its own propaganda. Humanity is ever accessible to the Absolute. The thing which we conceive to be true, we cannot but embrace, though disaster, suffering and death be our portion with it. Therefore attack is better than forgetfulness ; contumely is better than silence ; persecution is better than worship ; if only with all these the idea be kept constantly before the mind.

"When our country is unfortunate," said a European the other day, "the duty of the individual is to renounce his own career, and work for her only." What the speaker meant, was the *personal* career, the work that brings happiness, wealth, and position. Devotion to the impersonal idea often creates a career, but it is one for which we pay heavily in poverty, hard work, and sometimes final catastrophe and failure. Only the apprehension of some infinite good to be attained by this, for ourselves or for others, could nerve us to such a choice. For this, we have to wake in ourselves the great appetites. The *sannyasin* thirsts for renunciation. Let us so thirst for knowledge, for truth, for justice or for strength. Let us long to help and to save, even as children in the dark cry out for help. Realizing that only by the laborious climb towards the highest we perceive, can we be wholly helpful, let us work, work, work, to reach the Absolute Good in whatever path we seek to make our own. And above all, let us pray ever the ancient prayer of the Hebrew Scriptures—"Show Thy servants Thy work, O Lord, and their children Thy glory!"

But while the appetite grows strong in us, let us not be content with the first satisfaction that comes to our hand. Headstrong activity makes bitterness of failure. How often do we meet the man who wails and wrings his hands, because his efforts for the good of the world are not immediately rewarded! This is not true charity. This is but impulse, full of *tamas*. Long work, long thought, long growth of wisdom, are necessary, ere that man can strike the blows that count. And for such wisdom, we must have experience, and for such experience, again,—work.

> "Sharp as the blade of a razor, long and distant,
> And the way so hard to find!
> Such the sages have declared it.
> Yet do not despair! Awake! Arise!
> Struggle on! and stop not till the goal is reached!"

THE TEACHER.

THE true teacher knows that no one can really aid another. No one can rightly do for another what that other ought to do for himself. All that we can do is to stimulate him to help himself, and remove from his path the real obstacles to his doing so.

The taught, moreover, must develop along his own path. He must advance towards his own end. No one can develop along another's road, in order to reach that other's goal. The first need of the teacher, therefore, is to enter into the consciousness of the taught, to understand where he is and towards what he is progressing. Without this, there can be no lesson.

The act of education must always be initiated by the taught, not by the teacher. Some spontaneous action of the mind or body of the learner gives the signal, and the wise teacher takes advantage of this, in accordance with known laws of mind, in order to develop the power of action further. If however there is no initial activity of the pupil, the lesson might as well be given to wood or brick. Education or evolution must always begin with some spontaneous self-activity.

The laws of thought are definite. Mental action is not erratic or incalculable, a gust here, a whirlwind there. No: thought is always the outcome of concrete experience. A given sequence and intensity of action finding form and application on subtler and finer planes of reality, is thought. And just as water rises to its own level, so all our past determines the height to which our unresting thought shall wing its way. Inevitable is its rise so far, but at what infinite cost of toil and faith is won the next few feet of ascent in the clear atmosphere of knowledge!

To those who are accustomed to think in this way, the doctrine of reincarnation becomes a necessity. It is impossible to extinguish a mind, impossible to arrest the cycles of thought. The same force, the same knowledge will go on eternally finding new expressions. Or it will deepen and intensify. It cannot be destroyed. But it can be lost. It can be forgotten. Man is ever divine, ever the embodied *Atman* of the Universe. But he can lose sight of his high heritage, and though its potentiality may remain with him ever, as a possibility of recovery, yet in tilling the fields or scouring the cooking-pots its actuality may have vanished.

Spirituality comes to one soul at a time. Intellectual labour prepares the soil of millions for the whispers of truth. Intellect is the open door to the socializing of great realization. Therefore is mental toil a duty. Right belief is a duty. The highest achievements of the mind are a *Sâdhanâ*. We must be true to Truth. We must be greedy of wide views. Education to the utmost of which we are capable is the first of human rights. It was not the form of his knowledge but its selflessness, that made man a *rishi*. That man who has followed any kind of knowledge to its highest point is a *rishi*. If he had cared for money or pleasure, he could not have spent himself on labour that might have ended in nothing. If he had wanted name or fame, he would have gone far enough to tell what the world wanted to hear, and there he would have stopped. But he went to the *utmost.* This was because he wanted *truth.* The man who sees truth directly is a *jnâni.* This truth may take the form of geography. Elisée Reclus, writing his Universal Geography, and trying to give his highest results to the working-men of Brussels, was a *jnâni*, as truly as any saint who ever lived. His knowledge was for the sake of knowledge : his enjoyment of his knowledge was selfless : and when he died the modern world lost a saint. The truth may take the form of history or science, or the study of society. Would any one who has read the "Origin of Species," deny to Charles Darwin the place of a great sage? Kropotkin, living in a workman's cottage in England, and working breathlessly to help men to new forms of mutual aid,—is he not one of the apostles?

It is in India, aided by the doctrine of *Advaita*, that we ought to know better than in any other land the value of all this. Here alone does our religion itself teach us that not only that which is *called* God IS Good. It is the vision of Unity that is the goal, and any path by which man may reach to this is a religion. Thus the elements of mathematics are to the full as sacred as the stanzas of the Mahabharata. A knowledge of physics is as holy as a knowledge of the *Shâstras.* The truths of historical science are as desirable as the beliefs of tradition.

In order to manifest this great ideal of the *Sanathan Dharma*, we must try to set alight once more amongst us the fires of lofty intellectual ambitions. The great cannot be destroyed, but it can be obscured by the little. We must fight against this. We must remember the passion of those who seek truth for its own sake. They cannot stop short in learning. Did any ever stop short in the struggle for spirituality, saying now he had enough? Such a man was never a seeker of spirituality. The same is true of all intellectual pursuits. The man who has ever experienced the thirst for knowledge, can never stop short. If one step has been taken purely, he can never again rest till he has attained.

We cannot be satisfied, therefore, till our society has produced great minds in every branch of human activity. *Advaita* can be expressed in mechanics, in engineering, in art, in letters as well as in philosophy and meditation. But it can never be expressed in half-measures. The true *Advaitin* is the master of the world. He does not know a good deal of his chosen subject: he knows all there is to be known. He does not perform his particular task fairly well: he does it as well as it is possible to do it. In the little he sees the great. In the pupil whom he teaches, he sees the nation and Humanity. In the act he sees the principle. In the new thought he finds himself nearer truth itself.

We are men, not animals. We are minds, not bodies. Our life is thought and realization, not food and sleep. All the ages of man—those of the Vedas and the heroes, as well as our own small lives—are in the moment called *now*. All this do I claim as mine. On this infinite power do I take my stand. I desire knowledge for its own sake, therefore I want all knowledge. I would serve Humanity for the sake of serving. Therefore must I cast out all selfishness. Am I not a son of the Indian sages? Am I not an *Advaitin?*

THE GURU AND HIS DISCIPLE.

WHEN the doctrines of Hinduism can be formulated with sufficient breadth and clearness, it will doubtless be found that they furnish a key to the laws of thought in all directions. For the emancipation of man by his induction into constantly widening ideas is the real motive of Hindu speculation, and is the unspoken effort in every scheme of learning the world over. The source of Buddhism in Hinduism is nowhere better illustrated than in the opening words of the Dhammapada: "All that we are is the result of what we have thought. It is founded on our thoughts. It is made up of our thoughts." In all the world, only an Indian thinker would have dreamed of basing a religious system on this solitary truth.

In the great body of observations which have become current in India as religious doctrines, none is more interesting or more difficult to unravel than that which deals with *Guru-bhakti.* That in order to reach a given idea, one must hold the mind passive to the teacher of that idea, at the same time that one offers him personal service, is a truth which has only to be tested to be believed. But we shall make a mistake if we think that it applies only to religious teaching, just as we shall make an equal mistake if we call a man

 6 *

our *guru* for the simple reason that he teaches us a series of facts which have a religious colour.

We must turn a receptive attitude to all truth. We must be respectful to all from whom we learn. Age, rank, and relationship ought all to constitute claims on our deference, but nothing should win from us the deep passivity that we yield to character and learning. Amongst all who teach us there will be one whose own personality is his greatest lesson. He, and he alone, is the *Guru*. He alone represents that particular path along which our own experience is to lead us. But in everything that we make our own, even the most secular knowledge, we must constantly remember the source from which we received it. Every one that we meet must appear before us as a possible giver of knowledge. We should be on the watch for the *realizations* that each man has been able to reach. Thus a habit of attentiveness, respect for the knowledge and opinions of others, and an expectation of new truth, are all marks of one who is accustomed to mix in cultivated society. Nor can there possibly be a greater mark of vulgarity and want of fine associations than self-opinionatedness and forgetfulness of seniority in ideas.

Temptations to such errors meet young men at every step in a generation that takes up a new idea. The fact that they have departed from the paths of their fathers blinds them to the other fact that outside the special point of departure their fathers are apt to have greater wisdom than they; that even in the new idea itself they have their own elders and betters; that in any case, the idea is not worth much if it cannot deepen their appreciation of social cohesion and of the older culture they have left. Yet by such heedlessness and loss of delicacy a youth only succeeds in shutting the doors of fine society against himself. He is tried once, and allowed thenceforward to associate with his inferiors. His superiors find him intolerable. A young man with a hearty belief in his own leadership, is a social nuisance. The great impulses are calling for *disciples*, for martyrs, for trembling self-devoted service in which eagerness and humility bear equal parts. Those who are ready to offer themselves as *leaders* can be hired behind any counter or in any barrack. True leaders, we may understand once for all, are made, not born. They are made out of faithful followers. By much service, by deep and humble apprehension, let us hasten to their making.

The *Guru* puts us in touch with all that Humanity has yet reached in a given line. Through him, we enter into life spiritual and intellectual, as through our parents we received the human body. He represents to us all that, up to his time, could be known. It follows that the first of his qualifications was an unusual power of learning.

The real object of universities is to train the student to learn. The fine intellectual leader is he who learns most from a given circumstance. The power of passivity is the highest mark of education. This passivity, however, is not stupid or inert. It was not Arjuna alone who listened to Sri Krishna. His touch was felt and his words were heard by the delighted horses also. Nor must we forget that the sound-waves which make the Gita impinged upon the chariot itself. Chariot, horses, and man, all heard, but was there no difference between their three forms of passivity? Nay, two men will themselves hear differently. Nothing is more crude than an ill-timed activity. But the passivity that marks our advance is *intensive*, not idle, and contains within itself the fruit of all our struggles in the past.

It is the power of the *Guru* that is the force behind our realization. Whatever be the line of our effort, it would amount to very little if we had to go out into the wilderness and begin all over again, as isolated hints, the discoveries of man. Any significance that we have comes from our place at the end of the ages, our place at the dawning of to-morrow. This place is given us by our solidarity with the *Guru*, and by nothing else. The more we know, the more infinitesimal will our own contributions to human knowledge appear to us. The more we know, the more will history speak to us in trumpet-tones, the more full of meaning will the acts of great men become to us, the more shall we see ourselves to be striving with difficulty to see as our leader saw, to be making only a new attempt on his behalf.

On the other hand, the *Guru* makes no demands. The gift of discipleship is free. The *Guru* indicates the ideal. There is a vast difference between this and the attempt to enslave. Nay, there is none who so strives to give the freedom in which ideals grow and ripen as does the *Guru*. The disciple's devotion is for ever out-stripping anything that could be asked of it. In his own time the *Guru* ends personal service and proclaims the impersonal mission. But this is of his doing and not of his pupil's seeking.

The *Guru's* achievement is the disciple's strength, and this though it be the common ideal that is followed by both. Better to be no man's son than an original genius without root or ancestry in the world of the spirit. Quickly, how quickly, shall such wither away! They wither, and the men who set limits to their own offering never strike root. Which of these two is the deeper condemnation?

SELF-IDEALISM.

Of all forms of ignorance, few are at once so mean and so easy to fall into as that of self-idealism. How often, instead of aspiring upwards, we are merely worshipping our own past! Almost all good people are conscious of a great intensity of power and devotion in early youth. They are very apt to look back, for ever after, on the outside form which their life took at that period, and try all their lives to force that particular form on others. True freedom is a thing of which very few of us have ever caught a glimpse.

Self-idealism is a very special danger at the present time. This is a period of the recapture of ideals. We are always diving into the past in order to recover the thread of our own development. We exalt the name we bear. We praise our own ancestors. We seem to laud ourselves up to the skies. All this, however, is meant for encouragement, not for conceit. "Children of the *rishis!*" exclaims a great orator to the crowd before him; but if some common man derives from this the idea that *he* is a *rishi*, he shows his own *tamas*, and nothing more. This was not the reaction intended by the orator.

Similarly, when we say that Christ represents in Europe the Asiatic man, we mean the *ideal* of Asia, not any chance individual on the pavement. We must be careful to think clearly in this matter. Many persons propose for three hundred millions of people that they should practise the methods of Jesus, of Chaitanya, of Tukaram, and nothing, they say, could resist them.

Nothing could resist them! Of course not, if each one of us *were* a Chaitanya, or a Jesus! "As a sheep before her shearers is dumb, *so* He opened not His mouth," said the prophet of the Christ. But is *our* silence so eloquent as this? Only *tamas* makes this mistake! The methods of Christ will not bring the victory of Christ *to the man who is not Christ!* In him the dumbness of the sheep is mere sheepishness, not Christ-likeness.

Again says the *tâmasic:* "Let me wait for the victory, then, till I *am* like Him!" Very good, if self-engrossment were the way to become so. But unfortunately for you, it is not! Only the man *who forgets himself*, for the victory, can ever reach Christhood. Buddha died for smaller ends five hundred times, before it was possible for Him to become the Buddha! Each time He forgot Himself, forgot life, forgot death, became merged in the struggle, without a thought beyond. In the end He had earned the empire of the world, and had to renounce the certainty of that in order to mount the step beyond that made Him the vessel of compassion to the soul.

Each man has his own stepping-stones across the river of *Maya*. From stone to stone, one step at a time, we go. Our whole soul must be in the next step. Not for most of us to reach the Absolute now: for most of us only the immediate end, whatever it be, and for that, to forget self! Only through action can we rise to that which is beyond action. The world is full of causes for which a man may give his all. Ladders of rope by which we may draw ourselves up to the *Mukti* at present out of sight. Many souls, many planes; not for all souls a single gospel. Only through all runs the great law: by renunciation alone, by forgetfulness of self, does man rise to the Supreme Goal.

If we really forget self, any good-not-our-own will appeal to us. The good of others as an end in itself will become an appetite in us. We shall spend no time arguing as to theories and ideals, methods and plans. We shall *live* for the good of others; we shall merge ourselves in the struggle. The battle, the soldier, and the enemy will become one. Ours only the right to action, ours never the fruit of action!

But not as having already attained! Ages of strenuous activity are the opportunity of many to reach God-consciousness. We pant for the ordeal, we thirst for active service—not that we are already fit, but that by facing the cannon's mouth we may become fit. "By pouring himself like an oblation on the fire of battle, by remaining unterrified in moments of great terror, has Duryodhana attained to this felicity!" How knightly is the commendation! How heroic the path! "Things are not bettered, but *we* are bettered, by making changes in them," said the Swami Vivekananda.

So the world is a school, a gymnasium for the soul. Humanity is not a great hall of mirrors, in which a single figure is reflected again and again, here well, and badly there. God yearns to achieve Himself supremely, and differently, in each one of us. All that we may take from the pattern-lives is the law that guided them, the aim for which they toiled. Renunciation! Renunciation! Renunciation! In the panoply of renunciation plunge thou into the ocean of the unknown. Accept the exigencies of thy time, the needs of thy place, as the material out of which the soul is to build its own boat for the great journey. Think not that it can copy exactly any that has gone before. To them, look only for the promise that where they have succeeded thou shalt not utterly fail. Then build, and launch. Set out to find—Thyself! And let thy going-forth be as a blaze of encouragement to those who have yet to depart!

REALIZATION.

THE time has come when the Great Lives that have been lived in our midst are beginning to be recorded and written down for transmission to posterity. We can form some idea at this moment of the treasure that has been granted to the present generation, for which many in ages to come will long to have been here, or even to have looked upon the faces of those who possess such memories as ours. As we read, we belong at once to those who have seen, and to those who merely hear. We can share the feelings of both, at one and the same time.

In reading the Life of Sri Ramakrishna, one is first struck with his reverence for his own realization. Realization is the end and object of his life. Then he takes pains to protect and keep it. Yet he has so much! And we, who have so little, what do we do, to cherish that little?

It is told how he was one morning gathering flowers for the temple-worship, when it suddenly flashed upon his mind that the whole earth was a vast altar, and the flowers blossoming on the plants were already offered in worship at the feet of God. *Sri Ramakrishna never again gathered puja-flowers.*

What sacrifices do we make for the glimpses of thought and revelation that come to us? Every pilgrim after making a *tirtha* practises some abstinence in memory of the great journey. What memorials do we set up of the journeys of the soul? When the abstinence comes to notice once more, in the daily round, the pilgrim is reminded of the interior experience. He is wafted for a moment into the Divine Presence. So Sri Ramakrishna, looking at the flowers he would not pluck, was kept ever in the mood of that most vivid realization, renewing and deepening it from day to day. With us, the hurry and pressure of the little things of life soon crushes out of sight the great moments of the soul's life. It is the little things that matter to us, not the great! Why should the higher realizations be granted to us, seeing that we have so little room for them? Only at the end of long long struggle do we gain the least flash of knowledge. And when gained, what value do we place upon it? How long are we true to it? Verily, the lives of most of us are very like the footsteps of a man who climbs in sliding sand! What we gain we lose immediately, and, caught by new interests, are not even conscious that anything has happened!

No man can altogether escape the life of the soul. This is not the dominant, it is actually the *only* reality that surrounds us. The veil of the senses cannot fail to wear thin at times. We have but to set open the door and God streams in on every side. It is our absorption in the broken and contorted sun-rays of the body that hides from our eyes the Undifferentiated Light! When we become passive to it, when we allow it to shine upon us, when we are willing to make room for the One behind manifoldness, then we may find that the soul's life shapes all things. Life or death, happiness or sorrow, and the far greater destiny of knowledge or ignorance, are all determined by the spiritual energy. To this alone all else is plastic. By it all else is to be measured and interpreted. But there arises not only the question "What has one learnt?" but also that other, "What sacrifice has been made to keep this knowledge?"

PROGRESS.

"LOVE as principle, Order as basis, and Progress as end." In these words a great modern teacher—Auguste Comte—sums up his aspirations for human society. By him, with his view limited to the conditions of a single hemisphere, the idea of progress is postulated instinctively. The doubt of the East, that there could be any such thing in the end as progress, has not occurred to Comte. "Progress as end," appears to him an absolute truth. This is one of the more spiritual temptations of materialism, and of materialistic civilizations. When men have craved to place the end in happiness, or pleasure, or desire, then they are apt to declare that opportunity, that education, that amelioration of things themselves is the end. "Work for Humanity" sounds very grand as a declaration of one's object in life.

Here the pitiless analysis of the East comes in. Is Humanity, then, to be eternally in want of service? Is my beatitude to demand, as its essential condition, another's necessity? Is civilization capable, in any case, of expressing the infinite capacity, satisfying the infinite love, of the soul? Obviously, the service of man, apprehended as a motive in itself, is nevertheless only a means to an end, and that end is to be measured by the individual consciousness, not by anything outside. In other words, there is not ultimately such a thing as "social progress." This is an absolute truth. Let this never blind us, however, to the fact that, relatively to our own place in it, "social progress" is a very very real fact indeed.

For those in the life of the world, the aspiration after progress is a true and right aspiration. The world is a school for the soul. It is true there is a life beyond school, but this is best lived by him who has been faithful, heart and soul, in the life of the school, its work, its play, and its characteristic illusions. The *Grihasthâshrama* is the school of *Sannyas.* It is not the loose-living citizen who will make the noble *sadhu.* Quite the reverse.

Again, there is no absolute progress, perhaps, registered by Humanity as a whole. In the West, the progress of material luxury in one class is accompanied by the progress of poverty and degradation in another. The rise of Europe goes hand in hand with the decay of Asia. Apparent good is balanced by manifest evil, gain shadowed by a corresponding loss. Yes, but this very fact is in itself a battle-cry. There is no final progress, but there is oscillation of appearances. The rise of Europe cannot go on for ever, and neither can the decay of Asia. It is by contrast with its opposite that each gains momentum. If fall were not changed into ascent, by the energy of those falling, where would the power come from, for the counter-rise, later, of the opposite hemisphere?

Humanity is one, and each part of it is necessary to

all. The constructive ability of the Roman has as much meaning for the Hindu as the power and insight of the Upanishads have to-day for the Teuton. Relatively to space and time, Progress is a truth; and our most imperative duty is to live for it.

WORK.

ALL the Incarnations have talked of Work. What else did they come for, but to serve mankind? It had been far easier for them to have remained in the uttermost Bliss. By their eyes was seen at all times the vision of One-ness. Why should they plunge into manifoldness, and renounce the great joy, save by momentary flashes? It was all for man. It was all that others might reach their side. It was all that many might be made rich, even though the method should be by making themselves poor. Oh beautiful lives of the Avatars and Prophets! Wondrous mercy of the saints and teachers! How are we to make ourselves worthy of our union with you?

There is but one answer,—it is by Work. By stripping ourselves of ease, of privilege, of leisure. By emptying ourselves of self. By working for others, for ideas, and ideals. "As the ignorant fight, from selfish motives, so must we fight unselfishly." Our struggle must be as intense as that of the meanest miser. We must labour for the good of others as the drowning man clutches at a straw. There must be as much energy thrown into our renunciation as into most men's self-preservation.

How true is the monk to his vow! How he dreads the possibility of a fall! How unlimited are the sacrifices he dreams of, if only he may be found faithful at the last! Equally must we tremble and shrink from cowardice, from compromise, from failure in the task that has been laid upon us. Well has it been told us, by those who know life, that the world has no hell like that of having betrayed a trust that was laid upon us.

Do we desire above all things to fulfil our own ideal of integrity? Then what room is there for compromise? A compromise represents a mean found between opposite desires. If we have but one desire, what motive is there for compromise? Let each of us swear to himself that he will have nothing to do with any half-following, with lip-service, with weak-kneedness, and facing-both-ways. Let us throw our lives away, freely, gladly, as a very little thing. We would give fifty, if we had them, with the same royal glee.

Let us be true to our work. Our task is our *swadharma.* "Better for each man is his *swadharma*, however faulty his performance, than the task of another, though he could do it easily." That thing which faces me and frightens me; that very thing that seems the one most difficult; that beyond which I dare not look ——, there let me embrace Death!

"Right for ever on the scaffold?" asks Russell Lowell, "wrong for ever on the throne?" And then he bursts into his own answer:

"But that scaffold sways the future! and, behind the dim unknown,
Standeth God within the shadow, keeping watch above His Own!"

It is a grand gospel—this doctrine of fearlessness, of courage, of self-conquest. Arise, thou Great Divinity that liest hidden within us! In Thy name, all things are possible to us! Making victory and defeat the same, plunge we into battle!

But how are we to fight? Most of us, by work. The world's work is the great *Sâdhanâ*, wherein we accumulate character, by which, when the time comes, we can rise even into the *Nirvikalpa Samâdhi* itself. Character is self-restraint. Self-restraint is self-direction. Self-direction is concentration. Concentration when perfect is *Samâdhi*. From perfect work to perfect *Mukti*. This is the swing of the soul. Let us then be perfect in work!

REALIZATION THROUGH WORK.

THROUGHOUT history we may meet with instances of the poisonous effect on the human mind of ideas without *work*. The struggle with material conditions is eternally necessary to the upward growth of the spirit. When *Karma* has been exhausted, and the moment of enlightenment is at hand, this condition also must be held to have been transcended. But as things are, there are very very few of the human race on the earth at any one time for whom it is not essential that the whole strength should be thrown into concrete effort, into concentrated struggle, with the world about them. Only by this can there be progress in the idea itself. Only through this can there be growth of apprehension.

Work then is as necessary to the growth of the soul as is the Vedanta: perhaps more so. And work is at all times within our own power. The *bhakta* practises the ceremonies of worship. Work is the *puja* which a man offers to that Great Power which is manifested as Nature.

The idea, thought of as mere words, leads irretrievably to scholasticism and verbiage. Most serious of intellectual vices is a hair-splitting metaphysic. This may indicate the potentiality, but it can never be an actual manifestation of the power, of a mind. Left to run its own course, it proves the beginning of mental and moral disintegration. It has to be corrected and restrained, step by step, by the conscientious endeavour for the practical realization of ideas and ideals.

The world has known many great ages of faith. They have not, for the most part, been ages of inaction. The thirteenth century in Europe tended too much, it is true, to argument; but it was also the century of the building of splendid churches. Most of the finest of the cathedrals took their birth then. Similarly in India we are apt to overlook these truly great ages because they are not marked by the flames of war or the crash of falling dynasties. But the ages of faith are in truth the constructive ages, the ages of growth, of arts and industries, of the spread of education and the crafts. Great faith is above all things the concomitant and support of mighty action.

Again the trumpet-blast of truth has been sounded in our midst. Once more is our country waking up to that renewed apprehension of her religious wealth which has been the forerunner of every great impulse known to our history. The time may seem to us slow in coming, but it will assuredly arrive, when the influx of Indian thought upon the modern consciousness will seem to historians and critics the great event of these passing centuries.

Meanwhile, what of us? Are we to give the rich stores of our past, are we to enrich the world, and remain ourselves poverty-stricken and bare? If not, how shall we escape? If not, what must our course be? Our course must be REALIZATION THROUGH WORK. To the metaphysics of our theology has already succeeded the race-course of modern science. We have to throw ourselves upon this, and win our guerdon there. This is the task of our race in the world,—to prove the authenticity and grandeur of the ancient Indian wisdom, by proving the soundness and genuineness of the Indian mind itself, in that sphere of inquiry which the Time-Spirit has now opened up to all nations alike.

Amongst ourselves, however, there is another, and equally arduous duty. We have to share our knowledge as we gain it. This is the *Sâdhanâ* that will make our reading real. This is the practice that will turn it from mere words into actual knowledge. This is the struggle, sanative, concentrated, all-absorbing, that will give us new spiritual muscle, and add wings to our feet.

THE POWER OF FAITH.

ALL large systems of culture, of thought, of polity, need "beacon-lives," as they have been called, in which for a moment the innermost ideals of the communal aspiration are made real and visible to every man's understanding. And where the heart of a people is true and sincere in its striving, the great souls come. It was a critical moment in American history when the man Abraham Lincoln stood at the helm and embodied the national ideals. America may not always remain true to those ideals. She may seem to betray them in strangely complex ways. Yet nevertheless, freedom and democracy *are* her ideals, and no disaster that could befall her would be comparable in extent to loss of faith in her own sincerity in desiring to realize them.

The man who has thus lost faith in his own or his people's sincerity is known as a cynic. He stands aside and sneers at all effort, because it is bound to involve mistakes. He laughs at all feeling, because to his wisdom it appears childish. He makes light of prayer and hope, because he deems them to be hypocrisy. The cynic is the canker-worm of the corporate life. He openly avows his preference of selfish to unselfish ends and believes himself the greater for it. In ages of division and mutual antagonism cynics abound. In ages of great and united enthusiasm they cease to be. This is why large civic movements are necessary to the health of nations, whatever be the ends proposed by the movements in question. In the rush and flow of the mighty current, the emotionally poor, the morally barren,—those who would, without it, have been cynics—are swept up and carried on to ports that alone they could never have attempted to reach. Humanity is not yet wholly individuated. The crowd does not act as many: it acts as one, with a common heart and common mind. Nothing is more important than the power to form a single part of the great instrument, beating true at each step to its central impulse, apprehending what is to the interest of the whole, recoiling as by instinct from its insult or its hurt.

But this is a power which belongs wholly to the heart. The man who has it is like a little child, and because he is so, enters into his kingdom of heaven. He has never questioned the fact that there are in the world about him greater ends than his own good. He strives for more ends. Let the wise and prudent say what they will. He knows himself for a single brick in the great wall that is to be built, a single stone in the cairn to be heaped up. And where there is one man thus selfless, thousands more will come. The same causes that brought him into being will create his brethren.

The same unity holds good, as between *guru* and disciples, between leader and followers. The great *gurus* reach the vision of unity: their disciples struggle to attain it, by the conquest of manifoldness. But all these are one. The lowest of the saved is as much a part of the church as the highest of the saviours. In Vivekananda, for instance, Hinduism attains the realization of *Mukti*. And in the meanest task-man who follows him sincerely in the daily routine, she merely passes to the other extreme of the swing of the pendulum. The two are one. Their vision is one. Sincerity is the thread of their union,—the sincerity and childlike whole-heartedness of both.

Thus we are all one. To each man his own deed should be as sacred and as pure as to the *yogi* the meditation at nightfall. Is it English or Persian, is it chemistry or manufacture, that we would study? Whatever it be, it is holy. All work is holy. All deeds are revelations. All knowledge is *Veda*. There is no difference between secular and sacred. The modern history of India is as much a part of religion as the ancient. What! Shall Bhârata be a figure in the *Shâstras*, and the kings and leaders of public opinion to-day move outside? Not so. We are one. The highest and lowest of us, one. The oldest and most modern, one. Time is one. God is one. There was never a moment holier than the present. There was never a deed more worthy than that which I am set to do, be it weaving, or sweeping, or the keeping of accounts, or the study of the Vedas, or the struggle of meditation, ay, or the blow to be struck with the bared fist. Let my own life express the utmost that is known to me. However hard be the attempt let me essay the thing I think right. However bold be the effort required, let no great thing call to me in vain. I shall fail. Ah yes! My failure is the one thing certain. But let me reverence my own failure! I have the right to fail. Only by failure upon failure can I win success.

The world about us is sacred. It becomes unreal only when we have found a greater reality beyond it. Till then, it is of infinite moment that we should deal with it in manly fashion. Not succumbing to self-interest; not bribed by vanity or comfort; not enslaved by the mean ideals; so let us push on to the greatest that we know. And falling by the way, as most of us will fall, let us know that the attempt was well worth while. It was God whom we worshipped thus in Humanity. It was worship that we called by the name of work. The Calcutta lad who perished in a city-drain, in the vain attempt to save two workmen the other day, was as truly saint and martyr as if he had died at the stake for his opinions, or thrown himself down from the mountain-top in sacrifice.

THE BEE AND THE LOTUS.

IN the India of the Transition there is no word that seems to us more important or more *à propos* than the great saying of Sri Ramakrishna: "Bring your own lotus to blossom; the bees will come of themselves." All over the country are workers at forlorn hopes. Here it is a magazine, there a business. Somewhere else a man is working at science or invention. Again, he is doing what he can to organize some branch of industry or labour. Every one is confronted by perplexities that seem hopeless, by difficulties that appal him. Almost every one has to struggle against want of co-operation. All are striving to achieve success, without the tools or material of success.

To all in this position we would say, "Be not afraid! You can see, through the mists, only one step? Take that step. Plant your foot firm. You have done all you could, and to-morrow morning sees you fail? Expect that failure, if you will, but, *for to-night, act as if you would succeed.* Stand to the guns. Be true." There is not one who can command means. Rarely is a Napoleon born, to find all he needs for his task at his hand. And even he has been made through millenniums of exertion. All that we have at our own disposal is our own effort. "Bring your own lotus to blossom." Be faithful to yourself.

But there is another side to this picture. The bees

do come. The lotus feels no difference between to-day and yesterday. She knows not that at dawn her petals opened wide for the first time. She knows it only by the coming of the bees. The young athlete feels in himself no difference, of sterner control and finer adjustment, between the act of to-day and that of yesterday. *But to-day's stroke went home.* We do not know when success may come to us. Even now, it may be but an hour before we meet it. In any case, we work, we put in our full strength. When victory comes, be it late or early, it will find us on the field.

"Making gain and loss the same." This is not counsel for religious practices alone. In every undertaking it is the golden rule. Only he who can do this can ever succeed. But he who does, succeeds. No sooner does the mind steady itself on its true fulcrum-point of self-control than results pour in. It was our own confusion of motive, our own blindness of aim, that baffled us so long. Aim true. The arrow hits the mark. When his hour strikes, the bow Gandiva returns to the hand of Arjuna.

But we have to determine what is the effort to which we have a right. The will is like a great serpent. Not on its outmost coil is its striking-point. Nor on the next, nor the next. At the very centre of the spiral we find the deadly arrow. Rearing the head high, the cobra sees its mark, and strikes. We have to place ourselves aright, to poise ourselves on our own centre of equilibrium, to attain mental clearness. The schoolmaster would fain deliver his country, but he sees none on the benches before him who were made of the stuff of heroes. Let the schoolmaster teach as though he saw heroes. Let him arrive at clear thought and conviction. Let him educate with all his might, making defeat and success the same. The man who can do this will create heroes. He brings his own lotus to blossom. The bees come of themselves.

The potter yearns to deliver his people. Let him make good pots. The energy of his passion will make deliverers of the very men who stoke his fires. He thought to mould pots and vases. He was moulding men the while, out of the clay of the human will.

How strange that the lotus has to hear from the bees the news of its own blooming! So silent are the great spiritual happenings. Yet they are all-mastering. Events follow them. They do not lead. Means come to the man who can use means; always, without exception. Is victory or defeat my task? Fool! STRUGGLE is your task.

The higher and more responsible the duty before us, the longer shall we be in reaching it. And we must fight every inch of the way. In the end the deed itself may seem to be trivial. It lasts, maybe, only an instant. Many a soldier has paid with his life for the turning of a key, or a single flash from the gun. Yet to be in his place at that supreme moment had required all his past. A Gladstone, a Darwin, shows no extraordinary power save that of steady work at school or college. Maybe, the soul of him knows that the daily routine is for it, the army-drill of higher battles. Maybe, such have some instinctive consciousness of greatness. Maybe; maybe not. Neither he nor we can command our destiny. But we can all work.

We want higher ideals of struggle. The diver

struggles to find treasure. The miser struggles to win gold. The lover struggles for the smile of the beloved. The whole mind is set on the goal proposed. One of Sri Ramakrishna's great sayings, again, refers to the *châshâ* (cultivator) whose crop has failed. The gentleman-farmer abandons farming when he has experienced one or two bad seasons. But the *châshâ* sows at sowing time, whatever was his lot at harvest. However humble our task, this should be its spirit. Over and over and over again, the unwearied effort should be repeated. We should struggle to the death. Like the swimmer shipwrecked within sight of land; like the mountaineer scarcely reaching the ice-peak; so we should labour to be perfect in every little task.

Out of the shrewdness of small shopkeepers in Scotland have been born the Scottish merchants whose palaces and warehouses confront us on every side the whole world over. Out of the same experience was written Adam Smith's "Wealth of Nations." Even so the small and humble task is ever the class-room of the high and exalted. "Whatsoever thy hand findeth to do, do it with thy whole might."

THE LIFE OF IDEAS.

GREAT is the life of ideas. Men die that an idea may live. Generation after generation may pass away, while the idea on which they were threaded grows only the stronger for their decay. Let none, then, feel that in his own defeat lies any disaster to truth. A life given? What of that? Thought may be enriched by the death of thinkers! What is any one of us, unless the Infinite Light is seen behind and through him? And for the Light to be seen, may it not sometimes be needful that the vessel should be broken?

How often it happens that everything a man has believed is summed up and asserted in the moment of his death! Death consecrates. Death renders impersonal. It suddenly withdraws from the sight of others all the petty nervous irritations that have veiled the man's real intention, and he stands revealed in his greatness, instead of his littleness, before his contemporaries.

It sometimes happens that the greatest service a man can render is to retire. Great men must always take care to withdraw when the message is uttered. Only alone, and in freedom, can the child or the student or the disciple work out the idea that has reached him. The seed is buried while it germinates. The obscure processes of development would only suffer check from the attempt to watch and regulate. We seek ever to give birth to the greater-than-ourselves. But for this, it is essential that we seek not to see results. To give and die; to speak and leave free; to act, looking for no fruit; this is the great mood, that paves the way for the world-changes.

How many could throw themselves from the palm-tree's height? Those who are able to do this, having faith in truth, are the fathers of the future, the masters of the world, because only through them can the Impersonal flow in its fulness. Says a Christian hymn:

> "Oh to be nothing, nothing!
> Only to lie at His feet,
> A broken and empty vessel,
> For the Master's use made meet!
> Empty that He may fill me,
> As forth to His service I go!
> Broken that so more freely,
> His life through mine may flow!"

THE SHAPING OF LIFE.

IT will often seem as if life *hammered* the poor man, working him to that form which will exactly fill its place in the social setting, while the rich man, in the nature of things, is privileged, and allowed apparently to escape opposition. In fact, however, this hammering is experience, and is one of those the most important regards in which the buying power of poverty is greater than that of wealth.

Service, poverty, helplessness, are for strong natures great schools. It is only the man who is in a position at some time in his life to feel the full consequences of each word and act on the hearts of others, it is only that man who is able fully to explore the social consciousness. Only he whose single self-respect can exactly balance the respect that is due to others. For the manner and bearing of the subject should be different in form but wholly equal in dignity to those of the king himself. We ought so to serve that we might at any moment assume authority. This is the service that the great desire to have. He who longs to thwart and mortify the pride of the server invites defeat from his own subordinate.

The only bond that can knit together master and servant, sovereign and subject, officer and private soldier, is—not their personal relation, but—the constant subconscious recognition in every word and deed of an ideal of perfect conduct which both alike are co-operating to carry out. The man who *sees* the army, with his mind's eye, will not forget the deference due to his commander. And he in turn, being conscious that only as part of a great whole does he wield power, will be gentle and generous and winning in its use. When the moment comes for wrath, for condemning the disobedient man to sudden death, it will be this long habit of delicacy, and the fact that even now the claim is impersonal,—is made in the name of an *ideal*,—that will give power to the order, so that others will hasten to put it into effect.

For such maintenance of authority how much self-control is necessary! How complex an experience! In the brain-cells of the dispenser of law how long a memory must be stored up! Only such authority can be deep or enduring. It is a fact which anyone may put to the test, that only that man can maintain order who controls himself. Children, servants, and subjects are all alike contemptuous of the man whose own temper is not under his own command. And again, in order to learn the power of discipling others, it is first needful that we practise discipline within. Thus, authority and obedience are but obverse and reverse of a single power. The higher our education, the greater our ability to obey instructions. He who rules to-day obeyed yesterday. Let us so hold ourselves in obedience that to-morrow we may command. These are a few of the secrets of strong human combinations.

A man goes to a university, not that he may become a teacher, but that he may be *trained to learn*. He is best educated to whom all that he sees and hears conveys its lesson. He whose senses are open, whose brain is alert, he who is not deaf or blind—nor the man who has seen and heard most,—is truly educated. To the uneducated, the movements of the plant carry no tale. They pass all unobserved beneath his very eyes. To the uneducated, custom is an arbitrary and meaningless yoke. And the best educated man is not necessarily he who knows most already, but he who is most prepared to take advantage of what experience is bringing him. Thus every mental act prepares us for others. Every thought adds to our capacity for thought. Every moment of true concentration increases our ability to command the mind, and therefore the world.

How vast, then, is the moral difference between the man who applies himself to learning in order that he may lead the life of a scholar, and him who goes through the same course in order that he may enjoy advancement, or may earn money to spend on pleasure or luxury! The one is the son and beloved child of Saraswati Herself, the other is at best but Her hired servant. This is the distinction that is conveyed in those injunctions of which our *Shâstras* are so full, to practise love for its own sake, the pursuit of wisdom for its own sake, righteousness for its own sake. The stainless motive, that rises beyond self, ready to destroy the dreamer himself before the altar of the dream, —this is the only possible condition of true achievement. And this is why it is better to be born of generations of saints than of a race of conquerors. The conqueror is paid for his sacrifice. He spends what he has won. The saint adds his strength to that of his fore-goers, storing it up for them that shall come after.

NATIONAL RIGHTEOUSNESS.

INDIA is evolving a new civilization. New ideals and new methods have already made their appearance. Already she is projecting herself upon new developments in many different directions. The great danger of such an era is the loss of moral stability which it is apt to involve. For the aim and effort of civilization is always to maintain the supremacy of the moral faculty. And in periods of violent transition, the tendency is, by the breaking of old bonds and associations, to make the moral scum and wreckage of society come to the surface, and take the lead. The word "civilization" is a Western equivalent for our word *Dharma* or "national righteousness," and a nation may be regarded as having proved the value of its past, only when character has always been reckoned by it as the first of political and social assets, when the hypocrite has always been rated by it at his true value, and when the will of the people has spontaneously known to pursue good and avoid evil, all the days of its life.

No people can boast that they have shown these characteristics to perfection. This is obviously a race in which success is only of relative measurement. Yet the fact remains that if there could be an absolute standard for the appraisement of national and social systems it would be in terms of morality,—not in those of wealth or industry or even of happiness,—that that perfection must be expressed.

Morality is not to be understood here as the morality of social habit merely. The keeping of a time-worn law may depend upon our weakness quite as much as on our strength. True morality is a fire of will, of purity, of character, of sacrifice. It is here, and not to the expression, that we must look, to make the valuation of a nation's attainment. Yet some things are clear. When countries that have long preached a religion of renunciation,—a religion of the poor and lowly, of self-denial, of common property, of brotherly love,—when such countries are found suddenly to have abandoned themselves to the practice of exploitation—political, commercial, financial, or all three at once,—then we see a discrepancy between theory and practice, on which we can and ought to pass a judgment.

It is clear that a sound and true doctrine is not weapon enough for the will of man in the hour of a great temptation. Besides that of the truth or untruth of the doctrine held, there is also the deeper question to be considered of how far the nature of the man has been saturated with it, how far he has bent to it, how far he has assimilated it. Unless a nation be literally sodden with its religion, it is bound, when the opportunity comes, to throw it away in favour of self-interest. *And this is the defeat of civilization.* This is the true bar-sinister on the scutcheon of history.

At this point, however, comes in the question of the intellectual limitations of different faiths. Clearly, a code of religion and ethics which commands the ungrudging assent of our whole intellect will restrain and impel us more effectually than one that we are driven to regard as more or less an old wives' tale. Here we see the importance of a religion that is not discredited. And here also we find the secret of the failure of Christianity in the nineteenth century. Science, by dint of her mechanical inventions, has created a new world for Christian peoples to dwell in. Alas, that same science has also led to the scorning of the very Christianity which had been the great guiding and ennobling force in the world as they already knew it, and a Christian without his Christianity is apt to be an armed dacoit.

Christianity was not strong enough to include science. Is Hinduism strong enough to include the modern civilization? We answer yes! For towering behind the habits and practices of Hinduism lies that great generalized philosophy of the Vedanta, to which any religious ritual, any social scheme would serve equally well as area of illustration and experimental school. And from amidst the Vedanta itself, again, rises the *Advaita* of Sankaracharya as the peak of Gouri-Shankar crowns the long range of the Himalayas.

We are about to throw ourselves forward upon a great secularity. As a new development of Hinduism, in future, is to stand the Indian Nation. Instead of the *Samaj* and orthodoxy, the civic life. Instead of new worships and triumphant religious austerities, we are buckling on our armour to-day for the battlefield of learning, of co-operation, of self-organization. But what of that? Can the foundations of the *Sanathan Dharma* be shaken thereby? No, for have we not long ago been told, *Ekam Sat Viprâ Bahudhâ Vadanti?*

"All that exists is ONE. Learned men but call it by different names."

Does it matter that instead of ringing the temple-bells at evening we are to turn now to revive a dying industry? Does it matter that instead of altars we are to build factories and universities? Does it matter that instead of "slaves of the Brahmans" we are in future to write ourselves down as "slaves of the Motherland"? Does it matter that instead of offering worship, we are to turn henceforth with gifts of patient service, of food, of training, of knowledge, to those who are in sore need? If "All that exists is One," then all paths alike are paths to that Oneness. Fighting is worship as good as praying. Labour is offering as acceptable as Ganges water. Study is austerity more costly and more precious than a fast. Mutual aid is better than any *puja*. For concentration is the only means of vision—The One, the only goal.

O man, whosoever thou art who goest forth to work, in this hour of the nation's need, clasp to thy heart the weapon of thy service. Let mind and body be one in the act of labour, every muscle hard-knit, every sinew tense. Let all thy faculties converge on embracing the task. Let thy thought, day and night, be on that which thou hast taken in hand to do. Let *character* be thy supreme guide, perfection of service thy one dream. So shall there come an hour of knowledge. And the new age shall have added to the children of the Motherland the race of the saints of the market-place and the field, the heroes of the civic and the national life.

THE FLOWER OF WORSHIP.

THERE was a mood, to which we sometimes obtain a moment's entrance, when we hold in our hands an old book, an old picture, an old jewel, or even things as simple as a padlock, a piece of brass-work, or a fragment of embroidery. It was a mood of leisure and simplicity, to which the work in hand at the moment was the whole aim of life. The craftsman was concentrated upon his labour. The whole of *Dharma* lay in the beauty he was bringing forth. His craft was for the moment—or for that moment in the existence of humanity that we call a man's life—his religion.

Great things are always created thus. There is nothing worth having that has not cost a human life. Men have given themselves thus, for things that may seem, to the careless eye, to have been not worth the price. A single *vinâ* or violin—one out of the many required in the course of a year—may have cost all this to make. Patient search of materials, careful seasoning and mellowing, earnest study of conditions, infinite lavishing of work, all these are necessary to the instrument that will be perfect. But having them, there have been some that were as individual as human beings, some whose voices live in history. It has happened, often enough, that a man would give years of labour to the carving of a cameo, or the illuminating of a manuscript. Such things we think of as the possessions of kings, and we speak of them as *mediaeval.* That is to say, they are the product of ages like those of the European Middle Ages. But in India the Middle Ages lasted till the other day. Even yet we may see them persisting in humble streets, and bazaars, and in villages that lie off the line of railway. India is, as a whole, a mediaeval country. The theses of the Transition belong to her passage from one age into another, out of the Mediaeval into the Modern.

What, then, were the characteristics of the Mediaeval Age, that enabled it to produce its miracles of beauty and skill? It may be worth while to examine for a moment into this subject. In the first place, it had a great simplicity. A man lived, ate, and slept, in the room in which he worked. He was not surrounded by the multitudinous objects of his desire. His desire was only one. It was concentrated in his work. At the utmost, by way of ornament, he had about him a picture of some god, and a few specimens of his own achievements. Thus, his thirst after perfection fed upon itself. We do not often realize how much a great workman may owe to bareness and perfect simplicity of surroundings. To a certain extent, we may see this simplicity, any day, in the bazaar. The shopkeeper lives and receives his friends amongst his wares. Study, laboratory, living-room, all these are one, to the mediaeval man.

Another point lay in the fact that partly owing to the fewness of his wants, and partly to the abundance of food then in the country, the mediaeval workman was in no hurry to be rich. He could afford, therefore, to be lavish of time. The thing he made was, to a great extent, his only reward. Nor could he expect that to anyone else it would afford the enjoyment that he could derive from it. None else knew, as did he, the precise reasons why this curve or that colour had been chosen, rather than something else. None else could realize the feeling of rest, or gratification, or the sense of successful expression that rose in his mind when he looked upon it. He himself derived from his own work a pleasure that he never dreamed of describing to anyone, a joy that he could not hope to communicate. The work was done for the work's own sake.

Nothing tells so strongly and clearly in a piece of work as its *motive.* The desire for fame or money leads to qualities that destroy all true greatness in art. The genuine worker never asks for advertisement. He is contented to do well. Like the farmer of whom Ramakrishna Paramahamsa spoke, he returns to the task itself again and again, whatever be the discouragements that meet him in it. He strives with all his might, to bring his own lotus to blossom. What concern of his are the bees?

He works for sheer joy of self-expression, and his work is a joy to all he loves. Even the greatest things in the world have been made out of the happiness of such simple souls, who were contented to work as a child to play with toys. Cathedrals and temples, pictures and images, cities and kingdoms, have all been toys to the fashioners of them, working out of their own sense of things, even as a bird sings in the sunlight. The modern organization has upset many things which the ancient organization laboured to compass. Amongst others, it has made life complex. It has increased our needs. It has confronted us with many temptations, of which, in our old-time isolation, we knew little. The aimless desire for an accumulation of useless objects has seized upon us, and we do not realize that for this we have bartered what is infinitely more precious, the power of steady and absorbed work. For pictures on our walls, for sofas and chairs and round tables, for an air of luxury, and an infinite weariness of household drudgery, we have sold our birthright of dignified simplicity and a concentrated mind and heart.

Back to simplicity, and the lofty uses of simplicity! Back to the bareness that was beauty, and the depth of thought that meant culture! Back to the mat on the bare floor, and the thoughts that were so lofty! Let us ordain ourselves free of the means of living: let us give our whole mind to the developing of life itself. Not in the age of scrambling for appointments, and struggling for a livelihood, was Sankaracharya born, was Buddha born. Let the thatched hut at the foot of the palm be wealth sufficient: woe the day when Indian mothers cease to bring forth, and Indian homes cease to nurture, the lions of intellect and spirituality!

What the *sannyasin* is to life, that the craftsman must be to his craft, that each one of us to the task in hand. We must have a single eye to the thing itself, not to any of the fruits that come of it. We must keep ourselves simple, dependent upon no external aid, listening more and more as life goes on for that inner voice which is the guide to self-expression. In each line we must seek for that peculiar and partial form of *mukti* which is its goal. When *mukti* has been piled upon *mukti*, God knows if the Absolute shall be ours.

Five hundred times died Buddha ere he attained the infinite compassion. Shall we grudge a life, with its hour of toil, that we may feast our eyes upon some symbol of perfection? Shall we measure the devotion that, given without stint, is to make of us the *puja*-flowers laid before the feet of God? In a world of infinite variety the vision of Reality ends every road. Let us then push on with brave hearts, not fainting by the way. Whatever we have taken in hand to do, let us make the means our end. Let us pursue after the ideal for the ideal's own sake, and cease not, stop not, till we are called by the voice that cannot go unheeded to put away childish things and enter the city of the soul.

RESPONSIBILITY.

THE growth of modern cities in India shows that we are leaving behind us the organization of the undivided family, which once formed our largest conceivable social unit, and entering into still larger and much freer social combination. The city is one of the widest groups that can be formed. Nations are made up of citizens, and conversely, cities are the schools of nationality. A city is the most complex type of molecule, so to speak, in the national organism.

In a given molecule all the atoms contained are essential. Each atom, each sub-atom, and the relation of each to the rest, is integral to the whole. Can we say this of our cities of to-day? If not, they are not organized on a *permanent* basis. In mediaeval Benares, in mediaeval Lucknow, each atom and each series of atoms was essential to the city. In Conjeeveram and in many of our rural market-towns of the South the same is true to-day. Is it true of our modern cities, of Calcutta, Madras, Bombay? If not, the inessential elements will yet prove to be but temporary. They will eventually be cast out.

There is a difference between mechanical complexity and organic complexity. Those factors which do not belong organically to the civic complexus are the factors that cannot endure. And what is the test of the organic necessity of any given atom? The test that our ancestors would have accepted was *dharma*. Those who uphold the national righteousness belong to the city, belong to the nation; those who destroy and deteriorate it will have to go. The test of our cohesion, then, is a moral test, a test of character, of conduct, of uprightness. It is that particular kind of character, moreover, which makes large social combinations possible.

A study of such traits of character would then be valuable. Each of us, if we set ourselves to observe what these are, will notice different things. One will lay stress on good manners. There is no doubt that these are necessary, and that the standard will be much more precise and severe when we move in a circle drawn from all parts of India than when we lived only amongst our own relatives. Courtesy is a great lubricant to public life, and the delicate social emotions that make courtesy sincere and natural are one of the most precious gifts of humanity. Courtesy, too, may well be practised in the home. It is no excuse for a brutal manner that so-and-so is my mother or wife or brother. What then? Am I to be impertinent to my nearest and dearest, and reserve my best self for those whom I scarcely know?

Another will notice the need of punctuality, of order, of regular habits. All these are absolutely imperative in the civic circle. And all these are *Dharma*, for all mean self-control for the good of others.

We have to learn to be reliable, or what is called "dependable," in our dealings with others. *Responsibility* is God's test of man. We must be equal to our task. It is worse than useless, it is positively ruinous, like the uncompleted sacrifice, to undertake a duty that we do not carry through to its last syllable. The performance of duty, the social duty, the civic duty, is not to be allowed to vary with our own feelings, with our impulses, our tempers, even (up to certain necessary limits) with our health. "I am *responsible*" is a word that, uttered by oneself to oneself, should spur us to the highest effort, to the sternest sacrifice.

There is no reason for charity, for tenderness, for forbearance,—no reason that can be urged,—which is so strong as the *need* of him to whom kindness or gentleness is shown. And similarly, the most intense of all social motives is not ambition or self-interest, or love of fame or power, intense as any of these may be. The most intense of all motives lies in the thought "I am *trusted:* this duty or this need *depends* upon me." Here is the thought that makes the sentinel die at his post, that calls the fireman to the hottest point of danger, that rouses the slumbering spirit and puts spurs into the flagging will. And this is *Dharma.*

For examples of what is to be won by energy of social experiment, we are agreed that we must turn to the West. Even in the pursuit of ideas, while the *idea* is often better realized in India, its reflection in the social organization is better accomplished in Europe. These things are to be studied and contemplated. There is no solvent of error in conduct like true thought and right knowledge. We are of those who urge neither conservatism nor reform in social questions. We ask only for right *understanding.* And we hold that the temper of mind that will rush hurriedly upon either one act or the other is not conducive to true understanding, which needs above all things disinterestedness and calm.

Let us then compare the European solution of various problems with our own, and see, if possible, whether we have not much to gain from such consideration.

Even in religion, we find Indian worship a one-priest matter, while European ritual is a vast co-operation of singers, servers, ministrants, and others. In monasticism, the ideal monk of the East is a wanderer who goes free, from place to place, working out the personal ideal derived from his *guru*. He is often the embodiment of great and sometimes of supreme individual illumination. But he never has the discipline of the member of a close-knit organization, in which obedience is practised as a mortification, and punctuality, order, and business habits are rigorously imposed. Yet so completely has the monastic formation been assimilated by the West as a social institution, that such words as *abbot*, *prior*, *novice*, *refectory*, *cloister*, *bands*, *vespers*, and others, are now part of the common language, each with its precise meaning expressed and understood by all members of society alike. It was the organization of the great religious orders, moreover,—the Cistercians practising agriculture, the Dominicans and Jesuits giving education, the Franciscans acting as moral and religious missioners, a sort of mediaeval Salvation Army,—that made the modern organization of hospitals, red-cross sisterhoods, and relief associations in general, a possibility. It was their work in education that laid the foundations of all the universities and common schools in Europe.

But we have monasteries in India also. What is the distinguishing characteristic of the European? The distinguishing characteristic of European monasticism is its system, its organization, its clear and well-defined division of responsibilities. One man is the head. Under him may be the prior and even a sub-prior. One man trains novices; another attends to guests. However many persons live under one roof, there is no overlapping of functions, no repetition of offices. There is not one hour of the day that has not its appointed duty. The body monastic is close-knit, coherent, organic, and a degree of obedience to superiors is required of every member which is not surpassed by that of an army occupying hostile territory.

Developments like these, taking many centuries to perfect, have furnished that thought material, those conceptions of character and conduct, out of which the great commercial and industrial organizations of the present age have been constructed. Society is really one, and the experiments made by each part become the knowledge of the whole.

Behind every mental realization, however, whether of individuals or of societies, always stands some concrete experience. What was the concrete experience that so worked itself into the very nerves and blood of European races that their idea of a working-unity became so definite and differentiated? It is said by sociologists that this concrete experience was the conquest of the ocean. European peoples are coast-line-dwellers. Their conception of organization is furnished by the crew of a ship, and their temptation—incidentally, not only their temptation, but also their characteristic vice—is piracy. In the crew of the ship, the family—with the father as captain, eldest son first mate, second son as second mate, younger sons and nephews as working sailors, and so on—becomes transformed into the complex human working-unit, the social instrument, whose unity and discipline are tested for life or for death in every gale that the fishing-smack encounters.

In India and the East generally, it is supposed, in similar fashion, that the great concrete experience on which the national character is built, and by which its potency for co-operation is largely determined, is the rice-field. Here, it is said, whole families co-operate, under one man's direction, on an equal footing. They sow seed, they transplant seedlings, they harvest crops, without, say the sociologists, anything happening to call forth a great preponderance of ability in any one above the others. No special reward waits on ingenuity or inventive ability in the transplanting of rice. Every man's labour is more or less like the rest and of equal amount. Hence the firm hold obtained by the essentially democratic institutions of village, caste, guild, and family, in India. India is essentially a democratic country. Her monarchies and aristocracies are quite extraneous to her social system, and it is this which she has to thank for her stability and solidarity under experiences that would have shattered the unity of any less coherent organization. The only point in which India fails to stand comparison with the West is in the *complexity* of her social organization.

Benares is as beautiful as any mediaeval city in Europe. Indeed Europe has not more than one or two jewels to compare with it. Yet anyone who has seen a European cathedral will know what is meant by complex unity. The Western cathedral is not a mere building. It is like a Southern Indian temple—a treasure-house of carvings in stone and wood; of paintings on walls, on glass, and on canvas; of musical instruments; old metalwork; embroideries; libraries; and fifty other things. It represents, as many writers have pointed out, a *synthesis* of occupations, all held together by a single aim, governed by one head, united in the realization of a common design. And European cathedrals were the fruit of the sudden realization by the people of their own unity and their own freedom. For they sprang up in the great age of the passing away of the Feudal System and the birth of the great Free Cities of the Middle Ages.

If the complex unity of the ship's crew enable the European peoples to build cathedrals, the building of cathedrals, in like manner, has helped towards the modern complexity and success of industrial and commercial co-operation. For those who undertake great tasks and hold faithfully to their part in them, become possessed of great powers, and apply them unconsciously in every other function.

Let us also, then, undertake great tasks. Let us be faithful even in little things. A single wheel or screw may be small, even minute, yet a whole machine may turn on it. Let us be *responsible*, trustworthy. Let our word be our bond. The hand we have taken in ours, let it never fail for want of one to hold it. So shall every deed be the seed-plot of new powers. So shall every gain become the stronghold of a nation,

THE WORLD-SENSE IN ETHICS.

THE relation between the individual and the community, the extent to which no one of us is an individual at all, but merely constitutes an instrument carrying hands and feet and senses for the great social organism behind us, this is a subject on which we think too little and too seldom. Yet few questions are at the present time more important. A distinguished European sociologist has said that man in his earliest development thinks as "we," and only later as "I." The statement is not so paradoxical as it sounds. Most educated persons are aware that if a frog's brain be removed, and a drop of acid then placed on the hind foot of the frog, the foot will be rapidly withdrawn and the leg folded convulsively against the body. This is called "reflex action," because it is carried out without the necessary intervention of consciousness. Similarly, much of our social conduct, perhaps all that is a part of our characters, is reflex.

Imagine for instance, a slight put upon our family honour. Can we not feel the impulse of retaliation that is demanded of each and every member of the family alike, in the men as acts, in the women as malediction? Is such retaliation planned or instinctive? Can we not see from this something of what the European scholar meant? Is it not true that in family-matters we think even now rather as "we" than as "I"? And can we not see, casting our glance back over the evolution of humanity, that this must be more and more so, the earlier the period under review? In an age when individual scope was small, each man would be more true to the type of the family or the tribe, or the race, than in a later epoch, when, even physically, there is greater divergence of the individual from his kindred and brothers. Every state of society, then, and every social institution, carries with it its own reflex consciousness, its own code, its own ideals. Polygamy has its ethics, quite as much as monogamy. The European woman has her poets, as truly as the Oriental. Joan of Arc is also a saint, though so different in type from Sita.

Taking the whole of this reflex consciousness, these codes, these ideals, and putting together the principles of conduct which we can deduce from them, we call the result morality. Morality is fundamentally the expression of Humanity as a whole, through the individual. It follows that morality is not the same in all ages. It becomes finer and more complex, with the growth of intellectual knowledge and social experience. There was a time when the morality of family and tribe was all-sufficient; when it seemed right to a people to extirpate, in the name of this morality, not only the people of other tribes, but also their gods! Indeed as we look about us to-day, we may perhaps be pardoned if we think that that time, even now, has not altogether gone by.

It is the proud distinction of the Indian culture that Hindus have never, within historic times, been contented with the tribal morality, or the tribal ideal. This fact it is which forms the granite foundation of that destiny, in right of which India, as we believe, is yet again to lead the world. Even a philosophy like the Vedanta, even an ideal like that of Advaita, is organically related to the social experience, or it could never have been formulated. The day will yet dawn in this country, when young men shall set themselves to conquer all the most difficult knowledge of the world, with the sole object of being able to trace out these connexions between the communal organization and the national achievement. It may be that the caste-system, with its suggestion of a synthesis of races, ideals, and customs, was the concrete basis of that intellectual comprehensiveness which is yet to be the gift of India to the world. Or the secret may be found elsewhere. In any case, if we of to-day would prove ourselves the worthy children of our ancestors, we, like them, must refuse to be contented with a tribal morality. India may seem now to be but a trifling factor in the development of man, but it will not be always so, and great or small, none can measure the power of true thought, for the world is governed by mind, and not by matter.

Our *rishis* and *yogis* tell us of a stage of meditation in which we develop a cosmic sense, and feel ourselves to be present in the moon, the sun, and the stars. Far below this meditative experience, however, we must train ourselves and our children to another, which will assuredly help to fit us for it,—a *world-sense*. Through this consciousness, we must develop the power to suffer with the pain, and hope with the hope, of all men. All human sorrows are *our* sorrows, personally and collectively. Let us educate ourselves to feel them so, and then, in the moment of power it may be, we shall give birth to a morality which shall include them all.

In some such way has every advance in morality been made. First the trained sympathy, secondly the cultivated intellect, and third and last, the moral impulse, ending in a new institution, that cuts a step higher than humanity had heretofore reached, in the icy face of the mountain peaks. That is to say, all new social developments must arise out of new sympathies, new emotional experiences, giving birth to new and loftier ideals, and through these to a renewal or reform of institutions. Not by a mere substitution of one custom for another can a society be mended.

Such thoughts occur to us in connexion with the much-disputed question of woman's education. All that Indian women can do for themselves they would seem to have done. Forty years ago, we are told, they had still, for the most part, to learn to read and write in their vernaculars. All over India, spontaneously as it seemed, the effort began. The simple magazines which are so essential to first steps in such a culture-process found their way, by the cheap postal system, from the city-presses to the eagerly-waiting subscribers in the country. The vernacular education of Indian women was organized by the women themselves, and some very few well-wishers outside.

To-day, to a great extent, this vernacular education has been assimilated. In Bengal, Maharashtra, Madras, and the Punjab, every little girl expects to have to learn, not only to read her mother-tongue, but also to write it. This amount of wisdom is often attainable in the zenana itself, which thus becomes for the moment almost a schoolroom. In Bengal at least, such historical narratives as those of Romesh Ch. Dutt, and some of Bankim Chandra Chatterjee, have been read by all orthodox ladies, and there are magazines, and even illustrated magazines, in abundance.

But to-day we stand before the question of a new step to be taken in the education of woman, and it is meet that there should here be a certain searching of heart. Education is the highest and most moral of all social functions, and unless it is rightly directed, it may easily be made pernicious. Its direction, moreover, is more than anything else an affair of its motive.

What is our motive in desiring education for our sisters and daughters? Is it that they may be decked out in the faded finery of European accomplishments, and so take a better place in the matrimonial market? If so, the education that we are likely to give them is little calculated to help them over life's rough places. It is in fact, merely an extension of privilege, it is no enfranchisement, and perhaps those who receive it were better without it. Or do we desire to educate the women we are ourselves to wed, in the hope that their knowledge may save us trouble in the future? It is undoubtedly convenient to have a wife who can, unaided, take the baby's temperature when he has fever. If we go further than this, and feel that we should like to spend our lives with our intellectual equal, instead of with a prisoner,—bound to the treadmill of daily routine, and capable of few speculations beyond, in the darkness of the mental jail,—we are, even then, only men of taste, crying out for a more appetizing morsel than the common. We are not yet true advocates and champions of the education of woman.

The only ground on which woman can claim, or man assist her to obtain, anything worthy of the name of education, is that of the common humanity in both, which makes the one fit to be trusted and reverenced as the other, makes the one worthy of honour and responsibility as the other, and finally, makes the whole question of sex a subordinate consideration, like that of a blue or a green garment. For Humanity is primarily soul and mind, and only in a very secondary sense body. "Whatsoever things are just, whatsoever things are pure, whatsoever things are beautiful, whatsoever things are true, think on these things," is a text that has even more often cried for fulfilment by woman than by man. But how shall it be fulfilled, except in knowledge?

If woman is really as much a human being as man, then she has the same right to her fullest possible development as he has. If we should hesitate to emphasize the sex of man, then we ought also to hesitate at emphasizing that of woman. If we seek by every available means to ennoble the one, then we must surely seek equally to ennoble the other. The development of woman must be regarded as an end, and a sacred end. And this for the sake of woman herself, and not in any way as a mere accessory to the happiness or well-being of man.

CHARACTER IS SPIRITUALITY.

ONE of the most valuable generalizations of the modern era is that which was first arrived at, just about the time of the French Revolution, that *the individual, in his development, follows the race.* Each man and woman, that is to say, when perfectly educated, becomes an epitome of the history either of his or her own race, or of Humanity as a whole. This great perception made itself felt as a definite element in a new scheme of education, through Pestalozzi,—the saint and *guru* of teachers in the twentieth-century West. Pestalozzi saw that, if there were ever to be hope for the people, it must be through an education at once modern, that is liberal, psychological, that is founded on a knowledge of mental laws, and in accordance with the historic development of man.

The problem which the young student Pestalozzi, son and lover of the people, had to face at the end of the French Revolution, in Switzerland, was of trifling magnitude compared with that which confronts the son and lover of India to-day. And yet, in their innermost nature, the two are identical. For this, like that, consists in the difficulty of opening up the human field to a new thought-harvest, while at the same time avoiding the evils of mere surface-culture. The soil that has brought forth the mango and the palm ought not to be degraded to producing only gourds and vetches. And similarly, the land of the Vedas and of *Jnâna-Yoga* has no right to sink into the rôle of mere critic or imitator of European letters.

Yet this is the present condition of Indian culture, and it appears likely to remain so, unless the Indian mind can deliberately discipline itself to the historic point of view. To do this is like adjusting oneself to a new dimension. Things which were hitherto merged in each other all at once become distinct. That which till now was instinctive is suddenly seen to have a goal, which is capable, in its turn, of clear definition. The social and the religious idea, under Hinduism as under Islam, were in the past indistinguishable. Philosophically, of course, every tyro could detach one from the other; in practice, however, they were one, and could not be separated. For religious reasons, as was supposed, we must eat in a certain way, wear specified clothing, and fulfil a definite scheme of purification. Suddenly, through the modern catastrophe, the sunlight of comparison, contrast, and relativity is poured over the whole area, and we discover that by living up to custom, we have been not accumulating pious merit, but merely approximating to that ideal of absolute refinement, cleanliness, and purity, which is the dream of all fine human life, and which may as well, or better, be achieved by some other canon as by our own. Seeing the goal thus clearly, we become able to analyse and compare various methods; to add to our own conduct the virtues of others, and to eliminate from it the defects of all. Above all, we find out how to distinguish effectively between the social idea and religion. It is thus that it becomes possible to talk of "aggressive Hinduism."

Aggression is to be the dominant characteristic of the India that is to-day in school and class-room,—aggression, and the thought and ideals of aggression. Instead of passivity, activity; for the standard of weakness, the standard of strength; in place of a steadily yielding defence, the ringing cheer of the invading host. Merely to change the attitude of the mind in this way is already to accomplish a revolution. And the inception of some such change will have become evident to us all within a dozen years.

But before the first step can be taken there must be clear thought about essentials. The object of all religious systems is the formation of character. Theocratic systems aim at the construction of character through the discipline of personal habit. But at bottom it is character and not habit that they desire to create. No one will dispute that her ideals are a still prouder fruit of Hinduism than her widespread refinement. It is true that India is the only country in the world where a penniless wanderer may surpass a king in social prestige. But still grander is the fact that the king may be a Janaka, and the beggar a Sukë Deva.

Let us, then, touch on the comparative study of the value of habit as a factor in the evolution of character. We find in India that society watches a man all the years of his life, ready to criticize him for the hour at which he bathes and eats and prays, the mode of his travel, the fashion in which, perhaps, he wears his hair. To attempt a serious innovation on social custom in such directions as marriage or education seems to horrified public opinion not merely selfish, but also sacrilegious. And this kind of criticism becomes more and more powerful over the individual as the villages empty themselves into the cities. For the man who might have had the courage to make his mark in the smaller community would think it presumptuous to go his own way in the larger. Hence the aggregation of men tends to become the multiplication of their weaknesses and defects. It is the mean and warped judgment that gains fastest in weight.

But let us look at a community in which active ends and ideals are energetically pursued. Here a certain standard of personal refinement is exacted of the individual, as rigidly as in India itself. But public opinion, being strong enough to kill, does not stoop to discuss such points. The learning of the method is relegated to the nursery, where it is imparted by women. Having passed through this stage of his education, it is not expected that the hero will fall short in future of its standards; but if he did so, society would know how to punish him, by ignoring his existence. Both he and society, meanwhile, are too busy with other efforts to be able to waste force on what is better left to his own pride. For a whole new range of ideals has now come in sight. From the time that a Western child steps out of the nursery, it is not quietness, docility, resignation, and obedience, that his teachers and guardians strive to foster in him, so much as strength, initiative, sense of responsibility, and power of rebellion. Temper and self-will are regarded by Western educators as a very precious power, which must by no means be crushed or destroyed, though they must undoubtedly be disciplined and subordinated to impersonal ends. It is for this reason that fighting is encouraged in the playgrounds, the only stipulation being for fairplay. To forbid a boy to undergo the physical ordeal, means, as we think, undermining his sincerity, as well as his courage. But for him to strike one who is weaker than himself is to stand disgraced amongst his equals.

That is to say, a social evolution which in Asia has occupied many centuries is in the West relegated to, at most, the first ten years of a child's upbringing, and he then passes into the period of chivalry. Indeed if, as some suppose, the ten Avatars of Vishnu are but the symbol of a single perfect life, India herself has not failed to point this lesson. For after the stages of fish, tortoise, boar, and man-lion, are all safely and happily passed, and the child has become "a little man," it still remains for him to be twice a Kshatriya before he is able to become a Buddha. What is this but the modern generalization that the individual in his development follows the race? And in the last sublime myth of Kalki, may it not be that we have the prophecy of a great further evolution, in which Buddhahood itself shall plunge once more into a sovereign act of redeeming love and pity, and initiate, for every individual of us, the triumph of active and aggressive ideals?

Let us suppose, then, that we see Hinduism no longer as the preserver of Hindu custom, but *as the creator of Hindu character*. It is surprising to think how radical a change is entailed in many directions by this conception. We are no longer oppressed with jealousy or fear, when we contemplate encroachments on our social and religious consciousness. Indeed, the idea of encroachment has ceased, because our work is not now to protect ourselves but to convert others. Point by point, we are determined, not merely to keep what we had, but to win what we never had before. The question is no longer of other people's attitude to us, but, rather, of what we think of them. It is not, how much have we kept? but, how much have we annexed? We cannot afford, now, to lose, because we are sworn to carry the battle far beyond our remotest frontiers. We no longer dream of submission, because struggle itself has become only the first step towards a distant victory to be won.

No other religion in the world is so capable of this dynamic transformation as Hinduism. To Nagarjuna and Buddhaghosha, the Many was real and the Ego unreal. To Sankaracharya, the One was real and the Many unreal. To Ramakrishna and Vivekananda, the Many and the One were the same Reality, perceived differently and at different times by the human consciousness. Do we realize what this means? It means that CHARACTER IS SPIRITUALITY. It means that laziness and defeat are not renunciation. It means that to protect another is infinitely greater than to attain salvation. It means that *Mukti* lies in overcoming the thirst for *Mukti*. It means that conquest may be the highest form of *Sannyas*. It means, in short, that Hinduism is become aggressive, that the trumpet of Kalki is sounded already in our midst, and that it calls all that is noble, all that is lovely, all that is strenuous and heroic amongst us, to a battlefield on which the bugles of retreat shall never more be heard.

THE TASK BEFORE US.

It is small wonder if, in the act of transition from old forms to new,—from a mode of thought some centuries venerable, to one untried, and at best but modern,—it is small wonder if in the throes of so great a crisis, India should have passed through a generation or two of intellectual confusion. The astonishing phenomenon is rather the speed and ease of her re-adjustment. Within fifty years to have assimilated a new language, and that of an unforeseen type, and to have made changes at almost every rung in the ladder of ideal culture,—is this a little thing? Is it a fact that could be duplicated anywhere? To speak, in reply, of Japan, is mere foolishness. The problem of Japan, when midway through the nineteenth century, could hardly be compared with that of India. A small and compact people, of single origin, inhabiting islands and strong in their sense of insularity, could naturally mobilize themselves in any direction they pleased.

The trouble hitherto has been that the people were as passive to modern culture as to ancient. In a land where the segregation of the soul has been the aim of the highest thought and life, for thousands of years, it has not been easy to turn every energy suddenly in the direction of activity and mutual co-operation. At bottom, however, there is strength enough in India, and in spite of the demoralization of hunger and baffled hope, her people are about to set foot on the threshold of a new era. The ebb of the tide has already reached its utmost. The reaction of fortune is about to begin. That this is so, is due to the fact that at the beginning of the twentieth century the Indian people can take a bird's-eye view of their past history, and are able to understand clearly their true position.

There is a saying in India that to see through *Maya* is to destroy her. But few realize how literally this is true. The disaster or difficulty that has ceased to confuse and bewilder us, is about to be defeated. The evil about which we can think and express ourselves clearly, has already lost its power. To measure our defeat accurately is to reverse it. When a people, as a people, from the highest to the lowest, are united in straight and steady understanding of their circumstances, without doubt and without illusion, then events are about to precipitate themselves. Discrimination is the mark of the highest spirituality. Spirituality is the only irresistible force. Like the fire that wraps a forest in flame, is the power of the mind of a whole nation.

From the year 1858 onwards, there has been no possible goal for the Indian people but a complete assimilation of the modern consciousness. At that point the mediaeval order was at an end. Prithvi Rai and Shah Jehan, Asoka and Akbar were mingled in a common oblivion. Only the soil they had loved, only the people they had led, remained, to address themselves to a new task, to stand or fall by their power to cope with a new condition. Sharp as the contrast between the Gunga and the Jumna was the difference between the mediaeval and the modern. Invincible as the resistless current of the Bhagirathi is that new India that is to be born of both.

Up to the present, however, in the exhaustion of the transition, it has not been possible for the national mind to envisage the problem, so as to see or state its terms clearly. To-day this first stage is over. The Indian mind is no longer in blind collapse. It is awaking to fresh strength, and about to survey both past and present, that by their means it may determine and forecast its future.

What are the *differentia*, what is the precise problem of this modern age? Definitions are proverbially rash, but it is not difficult to state some facts and considerations bearing on this subject, with great precision. The outstanding fact about the modern period has been, undoubtedly, the geographical discovery of the world as a whole. The one characteristic of the modern mind, that makes it unlike the mind of any other age, is the completeness with which it is able to survey and define the surface of the planet Earth. The discovery of steam, with the consequent invention of railways and steamboats, has undoubtedly been the efficient cause of this exploration, and out of the consequent clash of faiths and cultures, has come the power to make the personal or mythological equation; to cancel, more or less to one's own satisfaction, all the elements of local prejudice in a given problem; and from this again has been born the ideal of modern science, of modern culture generally, the attempt to extract the root-fact from all the diversity of phenomena in which it clothes itself.

In this way, the intellectual and spiritual discovery of the world has followed hard on the physical or geographical. In culture, a new era has been proclaimed. It is no longer enough to know one thing well. It is also incumbent upon us to understand its place amongst other things, and its relation to the scheme of knowledge as a whole.

The pioneers of modernism, meanwhile, have been dominated by the ideal of the machine, to which they have owed so much of their success. To this fact we may trace our present-day standards of order and efficiency. A large house of business, with its staff, is simply a human machine of an intricate kind. It has been said that the Oriental regards his servants as personal attendants, the Western as so many hidden machines. Nothing could be more true. The Oriental is in every case an agriculturist, accustomed to the picturesque disorder of seed-time and harvest, cowshed and barn, and far from irritated by it. Every thought and habit of the Western, on the other hand, is dominated by the notion of mechanical accuracy and efficiency, and by the effort of the mechanician to achieve a given end by the most economical possible means.

In a society in which the highest knowledge fulfils the twofold test of order and synthesis, the great sin is provincialism. And here the new world differs from the old, in which the tastes of aristocrats were supreme, and mortal crime lay in vulgarity.

But while the great intellectual and social failure of to-day lies in provincialism, no serious mind assumes that the world-idea is to be arrived at easily. Only the tree that is firm-rooted in its own soil can offer us a perfect crown of leaf and blossom. And similarly, only the heart that responds perfectly to the claims of its immediate environment, only the character that fulfils to the utmost its stint of civic duty, only this heart and mind is capable of taking its place in the ranks of the truly cosmopolitan. Only the fully national can possibly contribute to the cosmo-national.

And this is understood to-day by cultured persons, all the world over. The cheap superciliousness of the young man who, on leaving his village in Kamschatka or Uganda, has been initiated into the habits and manners of the European democracy, and takes himself for this reason as an exalted and competent critic of his own people, only evokes a smile. No one desires his acquaintance, for he has nothing to add to the thought-world of those with whom he is so proud to have been associated. Every act, every movement, writes large across his forehead the word "snob."

On the other hand, to take one's stand persistently on the local prejudices of the village in Kamschatka or Uganda, is, though infinitely more manly and self-respecting, almost as futile. It is better to be provincial than to be vulgar, for our horror of vulgarity is the longer-grown. But both miss the effective achievement. What the time demands of us is that in us our whole past shall be made a part of the world's life. This is what is called the realization of the national idea. But it must be realized everywhere, *in the world idea.* In order to attain a larger power of giving, we may break through any barrier of custom. But it is written inexorably in the very nature of things that, if we sacrifice custom merely for some mean or selfish motive, fine men and women everywhere will refuse to admit us to their fellowship.

Cosmo-nationality of thought and conduct, then, is not easy for any man to reach. Only through a perfect realization of his own nationality can anyone, anywhere, win to it. And cosmo-nationality consists in *holding the local idea in the world idea*. It is well known that culture is a matter of sympathy, rather than of information. It would follow that the cultivation of the sense of humanity as a whole, is the essential feature of a modern education. But this cannot be achieved by mere geographical knowledge. The unification of the world has emancipated the human mind to some extent, and we now understand that a man's character is the sum of his assimilated experiences ; in other words, that his history is written in his face. And what is true of persons we see also to be true of countries. The very landscape is a key to the hopes and dreams of men. Their hopes and dreams explain to us the heritage they have left. History, then, is as essential to the modern consciousness as geography. It is the second dimension, as it were, of Truth, as we now seek it, naked and dynamic.

Our changed attitude changes all our conceptions. We make a new survey of our knowledge, and are no longer content to view dog as dog and cow as cow, but must needs learn all the links and developments between them. Their very differences are now regarded by us as a guarantee of their fundamental community of origin. We break open the rocks and scour the waste places of the earth, that we may find forms which will explain to us the divergence of horse-hoof from cow-hoof, reptile from fish, and bird from both.

Or we turn to the study of art and letters. Here again, our scrutiny has entered on the comparative stage. If we investigate the records of Baghdad, we must understand also those of Moorish Spain. It is not enough to follow the course of chivalry in France, unless we also assist at its birth in the German forests. Our idea of unity has become organic, evolutionary, and some picture of the movement and clash of the world as a whole is an overmastering need.

Yet even the finest mind is limited by its own ignorance. What a painful blank in modern culture whenever we come upon the word "China"! How little has it been possible to say about India to which any cultivated Indian can give more than a pitying smile! And how utterly misunderstood is the Mohammedan world! The world of culture, be it remembered, is not tainted by political corruption. Race-prejudice has no place in the ideal aspiration after knowledge. Why then should a silence, almost political, pervade the spaces that ought to be filled with Oriental interpretation, in modern thought?

The reason, as regards India, is easy enough to find. The Indian mind has not reached out to conquer and possess its own land as its own inalienable share and trust, in the world as a whole. It has been content, even in things modern, to take obediently whatever was given to it. And the newness and strangeness of the thing given, has dazed it. The Indian people as a whole for the last two generations have been as men walking in a dream, without manhood, without power to react freely against conditions, without even common-sense.

But to-day, in the deliberate adoption of an aggressive policy, we have put all this behind us. Realizing that life is struggle, we are now determined that our wrestling with the powers that are against us, shall enable us to contribute to the world's sum of culture, not merely to make adaptations from it. Our part henceforth is active, and not passive. The Indianizing of India, the organizing of our national thought, the laying out of our line of march, all this is to be done by us, not by others on our behalf. We accept no more programmes. Henceforth are we become the makers of programmes. We obey no more policies. Henceforth do we create policies. We refuse longer to call by the name of "education" the apprenticeship necessary for a ten-rupee clerkship. We put such things in their true place. We ordain ourselves intellectually free. What then is the task before us?

Our task is to translate ancient knowledge into modern equivalents. We have to clothe the old strength in a new form. The new form *without* that old strength is nothing but a mockery: almost equally foolish is the savage anachronism of an old-time power without fit expression. Spiritually, intellectually, there is no undertaking but we must attempt it.

Great realms of the ideal open for our exploration. New conceptions of life and duty and freedom; new ideas of citizenship; untried expressions of love and friendship—into all these we must throw ourselves with burning energy, and make them our own.

We must create a history of India in living terms,

Up to the present that history, as written in English, practically begins with Warren Hastings, and crams in certain unavoidable preliminaries, which cover a few thousands of years, and, troublesome as they are, cannot be altogether omitted! All this is merely childish and has to be brought to the block. The history of India has yet to be written for the first time. It has to be humanized, emotionalized, made the trumpet-voice and evangel of the races that inhabit India. And to do this, it must be re-connected with *place.* Calcutta, Madras, and Bombay, are the present view-points. Surely the heroes that sleep on ancient battle-fields, the forefathers that made for themselves the wide-walled cities, the scholars that left behind them precious thought and script, have laughed sometimes when they have not wept to see from high heaven the grotesque docility of their descendants! The history of India consists in truth of the strata of at least three thousand years. Ocean-bed and river-sands, forest and marsh, and ocean-floor again, lie piled one upon the other—and in each period some new point is centre. Ayodhya, and Hastinâpura, Indraprastha and Pâtaliputra, Ujjain and Delhi, Conjeeveram and Amaravati, what of the vanished worlds of which all these were born? There is no evangel without worship. Throw yourselves, children of India, into the worship of these and your whole past. Strive passionately for *knowledge.* Yours are the spades and mattocks of this excavation. For with you and not with the foreigner are the thought and language that will make it easy to unearth the old significance. India's whole hope lies in a deeper research, a more rigid investigation of facts. With her, encouragement, and not despair, is on the side of truth!

Great literatures have to be created in each of the vernaculars. These literatures must voice the past, translate the present, forecast the future. The science and the imagination of Europe have to be brought, through the vernacular, to every door. India cannot afford to imitate foreign institutions. Neither can she afford to remain ignorant of foreign ideals. The history of the past has to be re-written in simple terms. True hope for the time to come must fill all hearts, like a nation's Common Prayer. On the creation of such vernacular literatures depends the effective education of women.

Art must be reborn. Not the miserable travesty of would-be Europeanism that we at present know. There is no voice like that of art to reach the people. A song, a picture, may be the fiery cross[1] that reaches all the tribes, and makes them one. And art *will* be reborn, for she has found a new subject,—India herself. Ah, to be a thinker in bronze and give to the world the beauty of the Southern *pariah*, as he swings, scarce clad, along the Beach-Road at Madras! Ah to be a Millet, and paint the woman worshipping at dawn beside the sea! Oh for a pencil that would interpret the beauty of the Indian *sari*; the gentle life of village and temple; the coming and going at the Ganges' side; the play of the children; the faces, and the labours, of the cows!

[1] A rough cross of charred wood used to be passed from clan to clan in the Scottish Highlands, as the call to war. We all know the folded chapati of the Indian villages.

But far more, on behalf of India herself, do we need artists, half poets and half draughtsmen, who can wake in us the great new senses. We want men of the Indian blood who can portray for us the men of old, —Bhîshma and Yudhisthira, Akbar and Sher Shah, Pratâp Singh and Chand Bibi,—in such fashion as to stir the blood. We want through these to feel out, as a people, towards the new duties of the time to be. Not only to utter India to the world, but also to voice India to herself,—this is the mission of art, divine mother of the ideal, when it descends to clothe itself in forms of realism.

At each step, then, the conquest must be twofold. On this side something to be added to the world's knowledge, and on that an utterance to be given for the first time for India to herself. This is the battle that opens before the present generation. On our fighting a good fight, the very existence, it may be, of the next depends. Our national life is become perforce a national assault. As yet the very outworks of the besieged city are almost unstormed. Herewith then let us sound the charge. Sons of the Indian past, do ye fear to sleep at nightfall on your shields? On, on, in the name of a new spirituality, to command the treasures of the modern world! On, on, soldiers of the Indian Motherland, seize ye the battlements and penetrate to the citadel! Place garrison and watch within the hard-won towers, or fall, that others may climb on your dead bodies to the height ye strove to win!

THE IDEAL.

THE adoption of the active or aggressive attitude of mind changes for us all our theories. We sight now nothing but the goal. Means have become ends, ends means. The power to count the cost and hesitate is gone for ever. We seek great objects and create them, scorning small hopes. The India about us has become Mâhâ Bhârata, Heroic India. The future offers wider chances of sacrifice than the past. We look to make our descendants greater than our ancestors.

Words have changed their meanings. *Karma* is no longer a destiny but an opportunity. Do I behold injustice? Mine the right to prohibit oppression, and I do it. Before the honest indignation of one fearless man, the whole of *Maya* trembles and departs. Destiny is passive before me. I triumph over it. Strength is the power to take our own life, at its most perfect, and break it if need be across the knee. This strength is now ours, and with it we conquer the earth. No one is so invincible as the man who has not dreamed of defeat, because he has a world beyond victory to achieve.

Our desires have grown immeasurable. But they are desires to give, not to receive. We would fain win, that we may abandon to those behind us, and pass on. For that which is dearer to us than self, we long greatly to throw away our life, and this defeated sacrifice transforms all our work with energy. The whole of life becomes the quest of death. Those that are close to us become associated with ourselves in our risks and defiances. We learn to realize that in this fact lies their beatitude. Buddha did not sacrifice Yasodhara when he left her. He conferred on her the glory of renouncing with him.

Or is it *Brahmacharya?* This is not only for the monk. Nor is it wholly of the body. "Abstinence," says one, "without a great purpose, is nothing. It is only the loss of another power." But even *Brahmacharya* has to be made aggressive. Celibacy, here, is only the passive side of a life that sees human beings actively as minds and souls. Marriage itself ought to be, in the first place, a friendship of the mind. Exchange of thought and communion of struggle is far beyond the offering of comfort, and the one need not exclude the other. The *brahmacharya* of the hero makes marriage noble, for it seeks the good of another as an end in itself. In true *Brahmacharya* is involved the education of women, for a radiant purity comes to its perfect fruition in thought and knowledge and assimilation of experience, and there is a *brahmacharya* of the wife as well as of the nun.

In the life of *Tapasyâ* is constant renewal of energy and light. Every task becomes easy to the worshipper of Sarasvati. He spurns ease. Daily and hourly does the impersonal triumph in him over the personal. His ideal aspires upward like a living flame. Each circle reveals fresh heights to be gained. The wife shares in the ideals of her husband. She protects them, as if they were her children, even against himself. She urges him on towards them, when alone he might have flagged. She measures their common glory by the degree of this realization. Her womanhood is grave and tender like some sacrament of the eternal. "Not this, not this," is the cry ever in the ears of both. Counting happiness for self a little thing, each gives it to the other in seeking to bestow it on the world around.

Sannyasin, again, is a word charged with new significance. It is not his *gerrua* cloth, but his selflessness, that makes a monk. There may be monks of science and learning, monks of art and industry, monks of the public life and service, and monks for the defence of the defenceless. Great is the impulse of renunciation: greater is the *sustained* self-sacrifice of a heroic life. In the soul of the *maha-purusha* it is difficult, sometimes, to tell whether soldier or *sannyasin* is predominant. He combines the daring of the one with the freedom of the other. Years leave no mark on the aggressive life. It is as ready to cast itself down from the palm-tree's height, in old age, as it was in youth. Or more. For the spiritual will has grown stronger with time. Nothing is measured by personal hope or fear. All is tested by the supreme purpose, as making an end in itself. Self ceases to be a possible motive. The hand once put to the plough, it grows there, and the man would not know how to turn back. The *sannyasin* cannot be touched by misery. For him defeat is merely a passing phase. Ultimate victory is inevitable. He is light-hearted in failure, as in success.

Obedience to the *guru* becomes eager fulfilment of

an idea, and a seeking out of new ways in which to bring about fulfilment. Every act of attainment is now understood to be a spiritual achievement, and there is no rest without the handing on of each realization, as to disciples. At the same time, the standard of discipleship has grown inexorable. There is no passing of the spurious coin as genuine. The aspirant must serve, because without much service there is no germination of truth. He must worship, because without loyalty there is no manhood. But one stain of insincerity, one blemish of self-interest, and the *guru* must recognize—though to do so be like going maimed for life,—that this is not that *chela* for whom all *gurus* seek.

Love and hatred are now immense powers. Love, when no longer personal, when all strength, becomes rousing, invigorating, life-giving. Hatred is the refusal to compromise. It cuts off meanness and falsehood root and branch. Love, now, finds unity of intention behind everything that is sincere. Pride is too proud to found itself on a lie. The man is silent until he has first acted. Nor dare he boast himself of the deeds of his ancestors or the achievements of his fellows. A fierce humility mingles with all his ambition and tells him that praise from unworthy lips is sacrilege.

And finally the life's purpose has become a consuming fire. The object is desired for its own sake. Like Shivi-Rana, whose whole soul was set on sacrifice, the left side weeps that to the right alone it is given to suffer. Like Myer the German chemist, who had an eye and an arm torn off in the discovery of nitrogen compounds, the soul kneels in the midst of agony, to give thanks in an ecstasy that enough is still left to continue the search for knowledge. The vibration of the word Work when uttered by such workmen, carries the thrill of *Jnâna* to other hearts.

Strong as the thunder-bolt, austere as *Brahmacharya*, great-hearted and selfless, such should be that *sannyasin* who has taken the service of others as his *Sannyas*, and not less than this should be the son of a militant Hinduism.

GLOSSARY.

THE papers contained in this volume were written for an almost exclusively Indian audience. A brief glossary, however, is appended for the assistance of the European reader who may be unfamiliar with the Sanskrit words in the text. Sister Nivedita, in her occasional writing, adopted convenient spellings. Some of the words require, of course, a much fuller interpretation.

Advaita.	Literally, "One without a second." Absolute monism; one of the four principal schools of Vedanta philosophy.
Atman.	The self.
Bhajana.	Devotional song.
Bhakta.	One who has attained through devotion or love.
Bhakti.	Realization of the Divinity through love or devotion.
Brahmacharya.	Pupilage in divine knowledge during celibacy.
Brahman.	The one Existence, the Absolute.
Chela.	Disciple.
Gerrua.	The orange-coloured garment of the ascetic.
Grihasthâshrama.	The stage of worldly and family life—being one of the four stages into which a Hindu's life is traditionally divided.
Guru.	Teacher, spiritual preceptor.
Guru-bhakti.	Devotion towards the Guru.
Japam.	Prayer, with the telling of beads.
Jnâna.	Knowledge.
Jnânam.	Birth, life, incarnation.
Jnâna-Yoga.	Realization through knowledge.
Jnâni.	One who has attained through knowledge.
Karma.	Work; also the results of work. The law of cause and effect in the moral world.
Karma-Yoga.	Realization by a life of action or work.
Mahapurusha.	The Great Soul.

Maya.	The conception of the universe in its phenomenal (illusory) aspect, or as relative existence.
Mukti.	Deliverence; complete realization.
Nirvikalpa Samâdhi.	Super-consciousness, in which the consciousness of knowledge, subject, and object disappears.
Para.	Quarter (of a city).
Pranâm.	Bowing, salutation.
Puja.	Worship.
Punya.	Religious merit.
Rishi.	Sage; master of divine wisdom.
Sachchid-ânanda.	The three attributes of the Absolute: *Sat* (Being), *Chit* (Knowledge), *Anand* (Bliss).
Sâdhanâ.	Originally, the propitiation of the elemental powers for achieving a desired object or result; spiritual endeavour towards attainment; the life of realization.
Sadhu.	Saint, religious mendicant.
Samâdhi.	Super-consciousness, trance.
Sanathan Dharma.	Eternal religion.
Sannyas.	Renunciation of worldly life.
Sannyasin.	One who has renounced worldly life; a religious ascetic.
Sari.	The garment of the Indian woman.
Sloka.	A Sanskrit verse, a couplet.
Swadharma.	One's own duty—varying with the different capacities in which a man stands in relation to God, the world, country, state, family, etc.
Tamas.	Darkness, inertia.
Tâmasic.	Relating to Tamas.
Tapasyâ.	Life regulated on the practice of Tapas.
Tapas.	Fasting and other ways of controlling the body.
Thakur-ghar.	The household oratory; usually a small structure of wood or metal, in which the images are kept and the worship is performed.
Tirtha.	Pilgrimage, also a place of pilgrimage.
Tyâgi.	One who has renounced the world.
Vairagyam.	Renunciation.
Vedanta.	The system of transcendental philosophy so named because founded upon the latter part of the Vedas: conceived as embodying the ultimate aim of the Vedas. "The oldest name of the oldest philosophy in India" (Max Müller).
Yoga.	Literally, joining; the union of the lower self with the higher self.
Yogi.	One who practises yoga.

PRINTED IN GREAT BRITAIN BY THE UNIVERSITY PRESS, ABERDEEN